To: Stephanie
with love & thanks!
Gwen

All photos by Renée Anjanette except for those listed below.

Devon Meyers Photos:
End papers, book title page, inside cover, contents, gratitude page, introduction page, 14, 15, 37, 38 (left image), 41 (top image), 59, 60, 67 (left image), 78, 82 (both images), 89, 101, 104 (top right image), 109, 112 (top right image), 124–125, 129 (top image), 140, 158, 160 (top image), 163 (top left image), 172 (bottom image), 177, 182, 196–197 (middle image and right image), 202 (top image), 210 (top right image)

Author's Photos:
Image opposite contents listing, 68 (top left image), 72 (top left image), 77 (top left image), 150–151 (center image), 161, 163 (top right image)

Art Director: Nanette Furlong Bercu, StudioJPMS
Food Stylist: Louise Leonard
Prop Stylist: Amy Paliwoda
Editorial Director: Staci Amend
Proofreader: Bruce Taylor

ISBN: 978-0-692-28692-0

Printed in the United States of America

Welcome to Honeysuckle Hill

Celebrating Great Tastes and Family Traditions

Gwen Rogers

Photographs by Renée Anjanette

For Hannah

May you always find joy in continuing the tradition of celebrating life with family, friends and great food.

Contents

Gratitude

No project comes to fruition without a dedicated, talented and collaborative team behind the scenes. I am deeply grateful to the following people for their contributions: To the incredibly gifted photographic team that made the magic happen; Renée Anjanette, Joe Coonan, Louise Leonard, Devon Meyers, Tom Ordway and Amy Paliwoda. To Nanette Bercu for her artistic vision and creative genius on the book design. To Holly Vesecky and Rebecca Uchtman of Hollyflora for their exquisite, inspired floral design. To Staci Amend for her excellent editorial skills and amazing instincts, and to Bruce Taylor for his proofreading expertise. To Joanne Martinez and Monika Stout for pushing this through to the finish line. To my husband Brian, who so generously indulged my passion for this project, and to my mother JoAnne, the pilot light who not only sparked this idea, but who also helped to ensure that it was fully baked before serving. Thank you!

Introduction

I am a woman born of two vastly different worlds. My childhood in Michigan was pure storybook Midwestern; I grew up in a historic village often referred to as "The Town that Time Forgot." I reveled in the family garden, immersed in the bounty of every season—berries and vegetables in the summer, apples and crabapples in the fall—all transformed into steaming pies, savory casseroles and sweet jams. It was a slow and simple time, infused with the joy of planting and picking our own food... and the magic of elevating it to something else altogether.

Then, when I moved to Los Angeles after college, I suddenly found myself in a place without seasons or traditions, but with no shortage of trajectory. My career in the entertainment industry took off at a breathless pace, leaving me little time to connect to my adopted home and no time at all to consider the idea of family. And so, when I was eventually presented with the rare opportunity to embody the traditional role of wife and mother, I embraced it with some trepidation. Was I even qualified for this job? To my endless delight (and relief!), I found that I was simply returning to what I'd always known, and what was always in my heart.

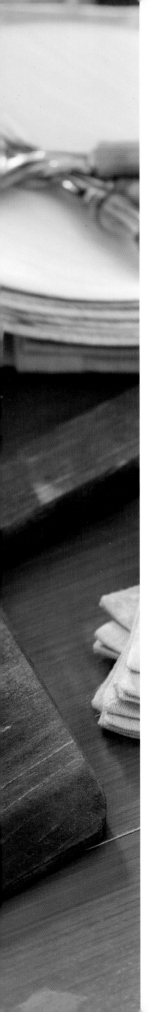

With this return came a related desire: to revisit the kitchens of my childhood. I am grateful to have grown up in a family of women who were not only truly talented in the kitchen, but also accomplished hostesses who took pride in making everything look divine and taste delicious. These women fully embraced their mid-century roles—they reveled in being housewives who, quite literally, catered to their families. Recipes were traded, tweaked, treasured. They were equally proud of their elaborate from-scratch conjuring skills AND their status as pioneers of the "can-to-table" movement. Entertaining was an art, and I was lucky enough to learn from true masters.

As my husband and I embarked upon the journey of raising our daughter, I began to search for a route back to tradition. We purchased Honeysuckle Hill, a historic home named and loved by the indomitable Bette Davis, which had gradually fallen into a "Grey Gardens" kind of disrepair. We rebuilt the house—and our lives—from the ground up. I planted a garden, battling the birds and squirrels for its daily spoils. I started collecting vintage embroidered linens, etched glassware, antique dishes and unique serving pieces. I started unearthing, organizing and reacquainting myself with family recipes, so that our daughter might inherit them one day.

And finally we began inviting people to enjoy massive, buffet-style meals at our home. This must be said: although my house has something of a pedigree, I do not. I haven't been to culinary school or worked at a fancy restaurant.

Our friends don't come to Honeysuckle Hill to try the latest trends. They come to share what is a terribly rare experience here in the City of Angels—an authentic, home-cooked meal.

Welcome to Honeysuckle Hill began as a nostalgic nod to the past; a way to introduce our daughter to her extended family through the simple, sustaining food they created generations ago. But to my surprise, it became something more: a creative, more connected way of living in the present. These recipes helped to marry my two worlds, and today our house in this notoriously transient city feels suspiciously like a home. I hope you'll consider this book an invitation to pull up a chair at our bountiful table. But most of all, I hope it will inspire you to create a unique bounty of your own.

Brunch

What's not to love about brunch? It's a meal designed specifically to move at the molasses-like pace of the best vacations—sated, slow and sweet. It gives us an excuse to bring everyone together for a relaxed, informal gathering that can, depending on the day, either kick off or wrap up a wonderful weekend.

Better still, the very word "brunch" suggests that a delightful, easy hedonism is about to take place. After all, it's two meals in one! It's the only meal that condones drinking before noon, and the only meal that makes dessert part of the main course!

Cocktails

Triple-Layered Sunrise Sips

Bellini Cocktails

Pastries

Sweet Monkey Bread

Fresh Raspberry Muffins

Cheese Piroshki

Cindy's Double Secret Banana Bread

Specialties

Cold Poached Salmon with Cucumber Dill Sauce

Brunch Strata

Baked Apple Pancake

California-Style Potatoes

Crêpes

Blintzes Casserole

Mushroom, Asparagus & Herb Quiche

Triple-Layered Sunrise Sips

1 (33-oz) bottle grenadine
1 pint orange juice, freshly squeezed
1 (33-oz) bottle tonic water

Use champagne flutes to serve this beautiful layered drink. You will need to ice a teaspoon to pour each layer into the flute in order to keep them separated. Beginning with the grenadine, pour over iced spoon until the layer is about 1 ½ inches high. Next, pour the orange juice over iced spoon until that layer is 1 ½ inches high. Finish by pouring the tonic water over iced spoon until that layer is 1 ½ inches high. Serve immediately. **Serves 6.**

Bellini Cocktails

With origins at Harry's Bar in Venice—where it was enjoyed in the company of regulars like Truman Capote and Orson Welles—is there any cocktail as gorgeous or glamorous as the Bellini? In 1940s Italy, white peach purée was seasonal, but today you can get perfectly tasty canned peach juice year-round. It's an easy, delicious way to add a dash of bella Italia to your brunch.

1 (750-ml) bottle prosecco
8 oz peach juice or peach Bellini cocktail mixer
1 fresh peach, pitted and sliced for garnish

Combine prosecco with peach juice in a pitcher. Mix well and serve chilled. Garnish with fresh peach slices. **Serves 6–8.**

Sweet Monkey Bread

Sugary, sticky and bursting with cinnamon flavor, this monkey bread is SO easy to make. The sweet recipe below is always popular at brunch—but I also make a savory version with butter, herbs and Parmesan cheese that is lovely with dinner.

3 (10-oz) cans refrigerated buttermilk biscuit dough
½ cup granulated sugar
1 tsp ground cinnamon
½ cup unsalted butter
1 cup dark brown sugar, firmly packed
3 tsp pure vanilla extract (I use Sonoma Syrup Co. Vanilla Bean Crush, available online)
¾ cup pecans (optional)
½ cup golden raisins (optional)

Preheat oven to 350 degrees. Grease a 10-inch round tube pan (or 10-inch springform pan). If using pecans and raisins, sprinkle half of the amount in bottom of pan. Reserve the remainder for use as you layer dough. In a shallow dish, mix together granulated sugar and cinnamon. Separate biscuits and cut each one into fourths. Roll each piece in sugar/cinnamon mixture and drop into prepared pan, layering until all the dough is used. If using raisins and pecans, sprinkle remainder throughout dough layers. In a small saucepan over medium heat, melt butter and brown sugar together and whisk until blended. Whisk in vanilla. Pour warm mixture evenly over dough. Bake for 30–40 minutes. Cool bread in pan for 15 minutes, then invert onto serving platter. **Serves 12.**

Fresh Raspberry Muffins

1 cup + 2 tbsp granulated sugar, divided
8 tbsp unsalted butter, room temperature
2 large eggs
1 tsp pure vanilla extract
¼ tsp salt

2 tsp baking powder
2 cups all-purpose flour
½ cup whole milk
2 cups fresh red raspberries
1 tsp lemon zest, for sprinkling on top

Preheat oven to 375 degrees. Line a 12-cup muffin tin with paper liners. Using an electric mixer, beat together 1 cup of sugar and butter until fluffy. Add eggs one at a time and mix well. Add vanilla, salt and baking powder and continue to blend. Use a spatula to fold in half of the flour and half of the milk and then add remaining flour and milk, gently mixing until just combined. Fold in raspberries until they are just covered. Use an ice cream scoop to place batter into muffin cups. In a separate bowl, combine remaining 2 tablespoons sugar with lemon zest and sprinkle a small amount of mixture over each muffin. Bake for 25–30 minutes until they just begin to brown. Cool for 15 minutes before serving. **Makes 12 muffins.**

Cheese Piroshki

This was the signature dish of my Russian great-grandmother—like her, it survived the revolution and continued to endure (and endear) on a new continent. This sweet version of her traditional recipe is that most often requested in our family, but she made an incredible savory meat-filled version as well.

FOR THE DOUGH
3 cups all-purpose flour
3 tbsp granulated sugar
½ tsp salt
½ cup Crisco®
¼ cup salted margarine
1 large egg, beaten
½ cup whole milk, cold
1 tsp pure vanilla extract

FOR THE FILLING
1 lb farmer's cheese, room temperature
4 oz cream cheese, room temperature
⅓ cup granulated sugar
2 tsp pure vanilla extract
1 large egg, well beaten
3 tbsp matzo meal

TO ASSEMBLE
4 tbsp salted butter or margarine, melted
6 tbsp granulated sugar
¼ tsp ground cinnamon
1 small can evaporated milk, for glaze

FOR THE FILLING: In a medium bowl, combine all of the ingredients with a spoon, cover and refrigerate several hours. When ready to use, divide filling into three equal 1-cup portions.

FOR THE DOUGH: In a medium bowl, mix together flour, sugar and salt. Cut Crisco and margarine into dry ingredients until mixture reaches a fine crumb. Add the egg, cold milk and vanilla to the flour mixture and combine with a fork, only until all flour is absorbed. DO NOT KNEAD. When a ball of dough is formed, cover bowl with a towel and let dough rest at least 1 hour for easier handling.

Preheat oven to 350 degrees and grease 2 cookie sheets. Divide dough into three equal portions. Roll out each third of dough on a well-floured board into a very thin rectangle—about 20 inches long. Mix together the cinnamon and sugar. Brush each rectangle with the melted butter or margarine and sprinkle each with 2 tablespoons of sugar/cinnamon mixture. Place cheese filling along one edge of the long side of the dough, then roll up tightly like a sausage. Using the side of your hand, NOT a knife, cut into 12 pieces. Turn each piece over and press with your thumb to form a round pastry. Place cut-side down on lightly greased cookie sheet and brush each piroshki with evaporated milk. Bake at 350 degrees for 25–30 minutes. **Makes 36 piroshki.**

Cindy's Double Secret Banana Bread

Cindy was my favorite camp counselor, and she ultimately became a lifelong friend. I knew I was her favorite camper when I finally convinced her to share her closely guarded banana bread recipe—or most of it, anyway. I know one of her "double secrets" is to whip the bananas and sugar together for five full minutes. The other remains a mystery.

4 bananas, overripe

1 ¼ cups baker's sugar (or superfine sugar)

8 tbsp unsalted butter, melted and cooled

2 whole eggs, room temperature

1 tbsp pure vanilla extract

2 tbsp crème fraîche or sour cream

1 ½ cups all-purpose flour

½ tsp kosher salt

1 ½ tsp baking soda

½ cup toasted walnuts (optional)

½ cup semi-sweet chocolate chips (optional)

Preheat oven to 350 degrees. Grease a 9x5x3 loaf pan or a dozen 3 ½-inch mini bundt pans. In a stand mixer fitted with a whisk attachment, whip bananas and sugar together on medium speed for 5 minutes. Add melted butter, eggs, vanilla and crème fraîche or sour cream. Sift together the flour, salt and baking soda. With a rubber spatula, fold in sifted dry ingredients until just combined. Add nuts and/or chips, if using. Pour into prepared pan and bake for approximately 1 hour until golden brown and a cake tester comes out clean. Let cool completely before slicing. If you are using mini bundt pans, adjust baking time to 20–30 minutes.

NOTE: If you do not have overripe bananas on hand, you can roast bananas in their skin on a lined baking sheet at 350 degrees for 20 minutes, turning once after 10 minutes. **Serves 10–12.**

Cold Poached Salmon

1 (3–4 lb) whole fresh salmon filet, head, tail and bones removed
1 tsp seafood seasoning
2 cups white wine
1 tbsp pickling spices
1 fresh cucumber, for garnish
2 fresh lemons, for garnish
Fresh dill, for garnish

Preheat oven to 375 degrees. Sprinkle seafood seasoning over prepared salmon filet. Place filet in heavy duty foil (large enough to seal completely over the fish) and pour white wine over it, then sprinkle with pickling spice. Seal foil and place in Pyrex® dish that is large enough to fit the whole filet. Fill dish ¾ of the way with hot water and bake for 25–30 minutes. When fish is finished cooking, remove from hot water bath, open foil and let fish cool to room temperature while sitting in the juice. Place in refrigerator for at least 1 hour to thoroughly chill before serving. Garnish with thin ribbons of cucumber, lemon slices and dill sprigs. Serve with cucumber dill sauce (recipe follows). **Serves 12–16.**

Cucumber Dill Sauce

¾ cup fresh cucumber, peeled and chopped to ¼-inch cubes
⅔ cup sour cream
⅔ cup mayonnaise
2 tbsp fresh green onion, finely minced
1 ½ tbsp fresh dill, chopped
2 tbsp fresh parsley, finely chopped
1 ½ tbsp lemon juice, freshly squeezed
½ tsp salt
Ground white pepper, to taste

Place prepared cucumber in a small bowl lined with a paper towel. Set aside for later use. In another bowl, mix together all remaining ingredients and chill for several hours. Add chopped cucumber to sauce just before serving. **Makes 2 cups.**

Brunch Strata

4 large eggs, beaten

2 cups whole milk

2 tbsp unsalted butter, melted

½ tsp dry mustard

1 tsp salt

1 tsp paprika

⅛ tsp ground white pepper

Dash Worcestershire sauce

Pinch cayenne pepper

8 oz sharp cheddar cheese, shredded or grated

1 cup cubed ham

2 cups day-old white or brown bread, cubed or torn

Lightly grease a 2-quart soufflé dish or a 10-inch springform pan. In a large bowl, whisk all ingredients together EXCEPT for bread, and mix well. Add bread cubes and lightly toss together. Pour into prepared dish, cover and refrigerate several hours or overnight.

Preheat oven to 350 degrees. Place pan in oven and bake for 45 minutes or until knife inserted in center comes out clean. Serve warm. NOTE: Also delicious with added fresh chopped herbs, bacon or cooked sausage. **Serves 10–12.**

Baked Apple Pancake

The trick to this tasty, ultra-traditional baked pancake is not what kind of apples you use—but how thin you slice them. Paper-thin apples will give you a perfectly puffed pancake every time!

2 tbsp unsalted butter

¼ cup granulated sugar, divided

½ tsp ground cinnamon

1 medium apple, peeled, cored and
     sliced paper thin

3 large eggs

½ cup whole milk

1 tsp pure vanilla extract

¼ cup all-purpose flour

½ tsp salt

Confectioner's sugar, for dusting

Sour cream or fresh whipped cream, for garnish

Preheat oven to 450 degrees. Melt butter in 10-inch omelet pan or oven-proof skillet. Tilt pan to coat with butter.

Combine 3 tablespoons of sugar with cinnamon and sprinkle over butter. Arrange apple slices over sugar mixture in pan. Cook until crisp-tender—approximately 3–4 minutes. In a medium bowl, whisk together eggs, milk, vanilla, flour, remaining sugar and salt. Carefully pour over apples. Place skillet on middle rack in oven for 8 minutes. Reduce heat to 375 degrees and bake for another 7–8 minutes or until golden brown. Remove from oven and dust with confectioner's sugar. Garnish with a dollop of sour cream or fresh whipped cream. **Serves 2.**

California-Style Potatoes

I like to use a combination of baby red, yellow and purple potatoes—but an old-fashioned Idaho potato can be substituted. The trick is to get your potatoes nicely browned and really crispy.

1 lb baby potatoes
2 tbsp extra-virgin olive oil
2 tbsp unsalted butter
2 fresh garlic cloves, pressed
1 yellow onion, chopped
¼ cup bell peppers, sliced into strips or chopped
      (I use a combination of red, green, yellow
      and orange)
1 Roma tomato, seeded and chopped
Salt, to taste
Black pepper, freshly ground to taste

Cut potatoes in half lengthwise. In large sauté pan, heat oil and butter together. Add garlic and sauté on medium heat for a minute or two. Add potatoes and cook over medium heat, scraping from the bottom of pan and gently mixing to brown on all sides. When the potatoes are golden brown and crispy—about 15 minutes—add the onion and peppers and cook for another two minutes. At the last minute, add tomato and cook for 30 seconds. Season with salt and pepper and serve immediately. **Serves 6.**

Crêpes

Crêpes may *seem* like a major undertaking for breakfast, but they're actually really easy to make. It's all in the wrist—just tilt the crêpe pan for paper-thin perfection! I still love them in their most basic form (with butter and confectioner's sugar) but cinnamon, fresh fruit and Nutella® all make delicious fillings.

1 cup whole milk
2 large eggs
3 tbsp unsalted butter or margarine, melted, plus extra for filling crêpes
2 tsp granulated sugar
1 tsp pure vanilla extract
½ cup all-purpose flour
Confectioner's sugar, for dusting

In a medium bowl, whisk together milk and eggs. Add melted butter or margarine, sugar and vanilla and whisk briskly. Slowly beat in flour until only a few lumps remain. Heat a 10-inch non-stick crêpe pan on medium heat. Dot with small amount of butter—when butter sizzles, pan is ready. Use ¼ cup of batter for each crêpe. Remove pan from heat, pour batter into prepared pan and gently tilt your wrist to swirl it around quickly and evenly to cover the pan. Immediately return pan to heat and let crêpe cook for about 2 minutes. Use a long spreader to gently lift and flip crêpe over. Cook for another 1–2 minutes. Slide crêpe from pan onto plate. Drizzle with melted butter or margarine and sprinkle liberally with confectioner's sugar, roll up and serve warm. **Makes 7 crêpes.**

From asparagus tongs to macaroni servers and sugar sifters, the Victorians had a separate ornately designed utensil for every conceivable purpose!

Blintzes Casserole

2 (13-oz) packages prepared frozen cheese- or blueberry-filled blintzes (12 blintzes)
6 tbsp unsalted butter, melted
4 large eggs

½ cup granulated sugar
2 cups sour cream
2 tsp pure vanilla extract
Pre-mixed sugar/cinnamon, for sprinkling

Preheat oven to 350 degrees. Pour butter into the bottom of a 9x13 Pyrex dish. Place a single layer of the frozen blintzes into prepared dish. In a medium bowl, whisk together eggs, sugar, sour cream and vanilla until frothy. Pour over blintzes and sprinkle with sugar/cinnamon mixture. Bake uncovered for 45 minutes to 1 hour. Serve warm. **Serves 12.**

Mushroom, Asparagus & Herb Quiche

1 (9-inch) pre-baked pie shell (see Thelma's Pie Crust recipe on page 165)
1 tsp extra-virgin olive oil
½ medium yellow onion, diced
1 lb fresh mushrooms, thinly sliced
1 ½ tsp salt, divided
2 garlic cloves, minced

½ cup white wine
3 large eggs
1 cup whole milk
½ cup heavy cream
1 ½ tsp fresh thyme, chopped
2 cups Gruyère cheese, coarsely grated
12 stalks fresh asparagus, washed and trimmed

Preheat oven to 350 degrees. Heat 1 teaspoon of oil in skillet over medium-high heat. Cook the onions until they have softened and started to brown. Add the mushrooms and ½ teaspoon of salt. Cook until mushrooms have released their liquid, the liquid has evaporated and the mushrooms begin to brown—about 10 minutes. Stir in the garlic and cook for another minute. Pour wine over mushroom mixture and continue cooking until most of the wine has evaporated. Set aside to cool.

In a small bowl, whisk the eggs together. Add the milk, cream, thyme and remaining 1 teaspoon of salt. Whisk briskly. Sprinkle half of the cheese on the bottom of prepared pie shell. Spoon mushroom mixture over cheese and cover with remaining cheese. Pour the egg mixture over everything. Arrange asparagus on top. Place quiche on rimmed baking sheet and bake for 30-40 minutes until edges are set but quiche still jiggles in the middle. Cool for at least 20 minutes before serving.

NOTE: Recipe will make 6 mini quiches in 4 ½-inch small tart pans or 1 large 9-inch quiche. **Serves 6.**

Spring Picnic

The idea of celebrating winter's end loses some of its relevance in Los Angeles, where the weather hovers amicably at spring-like temperatures year-round. But since one apparently can't take the Midwest out of this particular girl, I never miss an opportunity to unfurl my own version of the red-and-white checkered blanket.

Although our back yard is admittedly more formal than most, almost everything else about this picnic menu is intentionally casual. The food in this chapter is simply a slightly elevated take on classic American picnic fare. Every item is ultra-easy to make, to transport if necessary, and to serve in the great outdoors. And best of all, most of the recipes can be made ahead, so your day in the shade will be deliciously stress-free.

Refreshment
Old-Fashioned Lemonade

Snacks
Fire Crackers
Deviled Eggs
Peppered Candied Bacon
Homemade Pita Crisps with Assorted Tapenades & Spreads:
      Artichoke Spread
      Spinach-Basil Spread
      Olive Tapenade
      Sun-Dried Tomato Tapenade
Watermelon, Feta & Mint Kabobs

Bigger Bites
Asian Noodle Salad
Mom's Meatloaf
French-Style Oil & Vinegar Potato Salad

Treats
Lemon Squares
Thelma's Chocolate Chip Cookies
Grandma Jeanne's Brownies

Old-Fashioned Lemonade

1 cup granulated sugar
1 cup water
1 cup lemon juice, freshly squeezed (I use a variety of lemons from our yard)
4–5 cups ice-cold water
1 lemon, zested or microplaned
Fresh mint, for garnish

In a small saucepan, make the simple syrup by combining the sugar and 1 cup of water together. Cook over medium heat until the sugar is completely dissolved and liquid is clear. Remove syrup from heat and cool to room temperature. Pour syrup into a large pitcher and add lemon juice, cold water and lemon zest. Stir well and chill thoroughly for at least 30 minutes before serving. Garnish with lemon slices and fresh mint. **Serves 10.**

Fire Crackers

My adaptation of the Rooster's Famous Fire Crackers recipe—spicy, cheesy and absolutely habit-forming.

1 (8-oz) box saltine crackers
1 tbsp dried minced onion
1 tsp garlic powder
1 tsp onion powder
1 tsp crushed red pepper flakes
10 oz extra sharp cheddar cheese, coarsely grated

Preheat oven to 475 degrees. Arrange crackers in rows on an ungreased rimmed baking sheet, salted side up, so that cracker edges are touching each other and the entire sheet is covered. This will take approximately 40 crackers (5 across, 8 down). Sprinkle seasonings evenly over crackers, and then cover crackers completely with shredded cheese.

Place baking sheet in oven, close door and immediately turn oven temperature off. Leave crackers in the oven for at least 2 hours or overnight. Remove when completely cool. Break apart along edges into individual crackers. Store in airtight container for up to two weeks.

NOTE: Watch closely the first time you make these to see how your oven temperature runs—if crackers become too brown and start to burn, remove immediately and let cool completely at room temperature on the baking sheet. **Makes 40 crackers.**

Deviled Eggs

6 large eggs
3 tbsp mayonnaise
1 tsp prepared white horseradish, drained
½ tsp dry mustard
¼ tsp black pepper, freshly ground
⅛ tsp salt
Pinch granulated sugar
Paprika, for sprinkling

For perfect hard-boiled eggs every time, half fill a 4-quart sauce pot with cold water. Place eggs in water and bring to a boil. Continue to cook eggs at a moderate boil for 12 minutes, drain water and immediately plunge eggs into a bowl of ice water.

When cooled, peel eggs and discard shells. Cut eggs in half lengthwise and using a teaspoon, gently remove yolks and place them in a small bowl. Reserve egg white cups. Mash yolks together with mayonnaise, horseradish, mustard, pepper, salt and sugar until smooth. Fill pastry bag with egg mixture and pipe filling into the reserved egg white cups. Sprinkle with paprika before serving.
Makes 12 deviled eggs.

Peppered Candied Bacon

12 thick-cut bacon slices (maple-cured if available)
1 cup dark brown sugar
Black pepper, coarsely ground to taste

Preheat oven to 375 degrees. Line a large baking sheet with parchment paper. Coat each slice of bacon on both sides with sugar. Lay slices flat on parchment paper and using a spoon, pack down some additional brown sugar on top of bacon slices. Sprinkle liberally with coarsely ground black pepper.

Bake for approximately 15 minutes until bacon begins to brown and crisp. Watch carefully, as it will begin to burn quickly if left for too long. Remove from oven and let cool on parchment for 10 minutes. Using tongs, gently remove bacon slices and place on rack to cool completely. Bacon will continue to dry out and get crisper as it cools. Serve at room temperature. **Makes 12 slices.**

Homemade Pita Crisps

4 plain pita bread rounds
½ cup extra-virgin olive oil, in spray bottle or
    Misto® Olive Oil Sprayer

Sea salt, to taste
Dried mixed herbs, to taste

Preheat oven to 350 degrees. Use kitchen shears to cut around raised edge of each pita bread. Gently separate in half. Cut each half into 8 equal wedges. Lay flat but very close together, fitting as many as possible in a single layer on ungreased baking sheets and spray lightly with oil. Sprinkle with salt and herbs. Bake for 10–13 minutes, until lightly browned. Cool completely on a wire rack before serving. Can be made up to a week ahead of time and stored in an airtight container. **Serves 12.**

Artichoke Spread

1 (14-oz) can artichoke hearts, well drained
1 large garlic clove
2 tsp lemon juice, freshly squeezed

½ tsp salt
3 tbsp extra-virgin olive oil
Black pepper, freshly ground to taste

In the bowl of a food processor, combine artichoke hearts, garlic, lemon juice and salt. Pulse until well combined. While the machine is on, add the oil in a steady stream until mixture becomes smooth and creamy. Season with freshly ground black pepper to taste. **Makes approximately 1 cup.**

Spinach-Basil Spread

2 cups fresh spinach, long stems removed
1 cup fresh basil
½ cup raw pine nuts
¼ cup Parmigiano-Reggiano cheese, freshly grated
2 garlic cloves

Crushed red pepper flakes, to taste
½ cup extra-virgin olive oil
1 tsp lemon juice, freshly squeezed
¼ tsp salt
Black pepper, freshly ground to taste

In the bowl of a food processor, add spinach, basil, nuts, cheese, garlic and crushed red pepper flakes. Pulse until well combined. While the machine is on, add the oil in a steady stream and continue to pulse. Add the lemon juice, salt and pepper, and pulse again. Taste and adjust seasonings if needed. **Makes approximately 1 cup.**

Olive Tapenade

1 cup green olives, pitted and well drained

1 cup black olives, pitted and well drained

2 cloves garlic

2 tbsp roasted red pepper, diced

1 tbsp capers, well drained

3 tbsp extra-virgin olive oil

Crushed red pepper flakes,
to taste

In the bowl of a food processor, pulse together the olives, garlic, red pepper and capers. While machine is on, add the oil in a steady stream. Pulse again until just combined—the mixture should be chunky. Season with crushed red pepper flakes to taste. **Makes approximately 1 cup.**

Sun-Dried Tomato Tapenade

2 cups fresh basil

1 cup sun-dried tomatoes, packed in oil and well drained

½ cup Marcona almonds

½ cup Parmigiano-Reggiano cheese, freshly grated

2 tbsp Italian parsley

¼ cup extra-virgin olive oil

2 tsp lemon juice, freshly squeezed

Salt, to taste

In the bowl of a food processor, combine the basil, tomatoes, almonds, cheese and parsley. Pulse until just combined. With machine on, add oil in a steady stream and continue to pulse. Add the lemon juice and pulse again. Season with salt to taste. **Makes approximately 1 cup.**

Watermelon, Feta & Mint Kabobs

1 (8-oz) block feta cheese, well-drained
1 lb fresh seedless watermelon, rind removed
16 fresh mint leaves
2 tbsp extra-virgin olive oil
1 tbsp lemon juice, freshly squeezed
Black pepper, freshly ground to taste
16 small toothpick-sized skewers

Cut feta cheese into 16 (1-inch) cubes. Set aside. Cut watermelon into 16 (1-inch) cubes. To assemble, begin by spearing one cube of watermelon, add one mint leaf and then follow with a cheese cube. Repeat until you have 16 kabobs. Arrange kabobs on platter. In a small bowl, whisk together oil and lemon juice. Drizzle over kabobs and then sprinkle with a few generous grinds of black pepper. **Makes 16 kabobs.**

Asian Noodle Salad

2 chicken breasts, poached
1 (8-oz) package Chinese noodles
6 tbsp sesame oil
5 tbsp soy sauce
4 tsp granulated sugar
2 tbsp rice vinegar
2 tsp hot chili oil
2 garlic cloves, pressed
1 tsp fresh ginger, finely minced

1 tsp honey
1 tsp sesame paste
2 tbsp fresh scallions, chopped
Pinch cayenne pepper
1 tbsp crunchy peanut butter
    (optional)
Fresh snow peas, for garnish
Julienned carrot strips, for garnish
Crushed peanuts, for garnish

Discard skin and bones from poached chicken breasts, finely shred meat and set aside. Cook noodles according to package instructions. Drain well. In a medium bowl, whisk together all remaining ingredients and adjust seasonings to taste. Pour ¾ of the dressing on noodles, add chicken and gently toss to combine. Reserve the unused portion of dressing for later use. Cover and refrigerate noodles for at least 6 hours. Gently toss with remainder of dressing just before serving. Garnish with snow peas, julienned carrot strips and crushed peanuts. **Serves 6–8.**

Mom's Meatloaf

2 lb fresh ground sirloin
½ cup water
½ cup ketchup
Worcestershire sauce, to taste
Garlic powder, to taste
¼ tsp white ground pepper
1 tbsp dried minced onion
1 large egg, beaten until frothy
½ cup plain bread crumbs, scant

Preheat oven to 350 degrees. Lightly grease a 9-inch glass Pyrex loaf pan. Place ground sirloin in a large bowl. In a separate small bowl, mix water and ketchup together to make sauce base. Add Worcestershire sauce, garlic powder, pepper and onion and adjust seasonings to taste. Add beaten egg. Pour mixture over sirloin and gently blend. Add bread crumbs and mix until meat just holds together—do not over handle. Place in prepared pan and cross score top with knife. Bake for one hour. Cool completely, cover and refrigerate overnight. Slice and serve cold or at room temperature for picnic. **Serves 8.**

French-Style Oil & Vinegar Potato Salad

1 cup extra-virgin olive oil
⅓ cup red wine vinegar
2 tsp kosher salt
2 tsp granulated sugar
1 tsp dry vermouth
1 lb tiny whole potatoes in skins
¾ cup green onion, chopped
¼ cup caraway seeds (optional)

In a medium bowl, make the dressing by whisking together the oil, vinegar, salt, sugar and vermouth. Set aside. In a large pot, boil potatoes in salted water until fork tender (do not overcook or they will be too soft to slice). Drain potatoes. While potatoes are still warm, slice and place in large mixing bowl. Add the onion and caraway seeds if using. Gradually add the dressing, ¼ cup at a time, gently tossing with a rubber spatula. Serve at room temperature. **Serves 6.**

Lemon Squares

A family favorite from my mom's friend, Judy. These are the only lemon squares I have ever tasted that have exactly the right proportion of curd to crust—each delicate, buttery bite delivers the perfect lemony zing.

FOR THE CRUST:
½ cup unsalted butter, room temperature
¼ cup confectioner's sugar
⅛ tsp salt
1 cup all-purpose flour

FOR THE TOPPING:
2 large eggs, slightly beaten
1 cup granulated sugar
2 tbsp all-purpose flour
3 tbsp lemon juice, freshly squeezed
½ tsp lemon zest

Preheat oven to 350 degrees. In a small mixing bowl, make the crust by blending together butter, confectioner's sugar, salt and flour. Press crust into the bottom of a 9-inch square pan. Bake for 20 minutes. Meanwhile, make the topping: Use an electric mixer to beat together eggs, sugar, flour, lemon juice and lemon zest until blended. Pour lemon mixture over baked crust, right out of the oven, and return to oven. Continue baking for another 30 minutes. Cool completely before cutting into squares. Dust with confectioner's sugar to serve. **Makes 16 squares.**

Thelma's Chocolate Chip Cookies

There are two camps of chocolate chip cookie-lovers—the Chewies and the Crispies. Thanks to this recipe, I will always be in the Crispy camp! When we were little, family friend Thelma always made sure these perfectly crispy cookies were on hand for every special occasion. To me, they simply taste like home. Chewies take note: this recipe just might convert you.

9 tbsp salted margarine
7 tbsp dark brown sugar, firmly packed
6 tbsp granulated sugar
1 large egg
1 tsp pure vanilla extract

1 tsp water
1 cup all-purpose flour, plus 2 tbsp
½ tsp baking soda
½ tsp salt
6 oz semi-sweet chocolate chips

Preheat oven to 350 degrees. In a medium mixing bowl, use a wooden spoon to cream together margarine and sugars. Add the egg and mix well to combine. Add the vanilla and water and blend. In a small bowl, sift together the flour, baking soda and salt, and add to creamed mixture. Stir in the chocolate chips. Drop teaspoonfuls of dough onto greased cookie sheets (4 across, 6 down). Bake at 350 degrees for 8–10 minutes and cool on a wire rack. These keep in an airtight container for up to 5 days, in the unlikely event that there are any left. **Makes 48 cookies.**

Grandma Jeanne's Brownies

My Grandma Jeanne baked these moist and fudgy brownies for us when we were children. Despite my many attempts to upgrade them using French butter and gourmet chocolate, I ultimately found that the original recipe had no room for improvement.

4 oz unsweetened chocolate
8 tbsp salted margarine
½ cup Crisco
4 large eggs
2 cups granulated sugar
1 cup all-purpose flour
¼ tsp salt
2 tsp pure vanilla extract
Confectioner's sugar, for dusting

Preheat oven to 325 degrees. Grease a 9x13 baking pan. NOTE: If you can find a pan that has a removable bottom, this will make cutting the brownies much easier. In saucepan or microwave, melt together chocolate, margarine and Crisco. Let cool slightly. In a medium bowl, whisk together eggs and sugar until foamy. Add cooled chocolate mixture to eggs. Add flour, salt and vanilla, and mix with a spatula until just combined. Pour into prepared pan.

Bake for 25 minutes or until a cake tester inserted in center comes out clean. Let cool completely. For easier cutting and handling, freeze uncut brownies for several hours. Defrost for 5–10 minutes prior to cutting. Let cut brownies defrost completely before serving. Dust with confectioner's sugar. **Makes approximately 30 brownies.**

Although most outdoor meals aren't complete without a few real *ants, the insects pictured here are printed on our melamine picnic plates.*

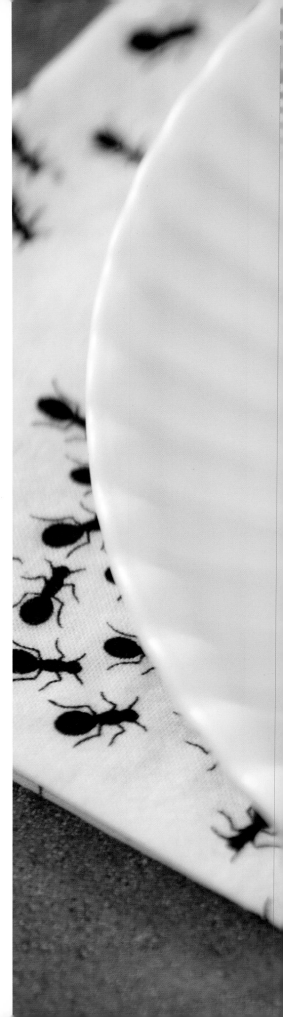

Birthday Dinner

Birthdays have always been a big production in my family—in fact, each one is *such* a major undertaking that I've often wondered why we limit them to a single calendar day! With each passing year, while other grown-ups have started to view this milestone with mounting trepidation, I'm more and more tempted to stretch out the festivities for as long as I can. Why not, I wonder, a birthday *season*? Or even a year-long birthday jubilee?

In any case, I've collected our family's favorite "big night" recipes here. Use this menu as a complete meal for birthdays and special occasions—make everything on one night, spread the party out over a month or even have a half-birthday, just for the cake of it! After all, birthdays are about celebration. And as with dessert, there's always room for more.

Starters
Baked Cheese Bites

Tuna Pâté

Marinated Shrimp & Artichokes

Main Courses
Roasted Rack of Lamb

Broiled Salmon with Tangy Tartar Sauce

Sides
Green Bean Purée

Cauliflower Purée

Mustard Roasted Potatoes

Sweets
Thelma's Old-Fashioned Birthday Cake
     with Fudge Frosting

Frozen Lemon Torte

Fresh Strawberry Pie

Baked Cheese Bites

This is a classic hors d'oeuvre from my childhood in the 1970s—these cheese bites are impossible to resist, and are still the best way I can think of to spoil one's appetite. Velveeta provides the creamiest texture, but cheddar will work nicely as well.

8 oz Velveeta® cheese, cubed (or mild cheddar cheese, coarsely grated), room temperature
¼ cup unsalted butter or margarine, room temperature
1 cup all-purpose flour
½ tsp salt
¼ tsp onion powder
Pinch cayenne pepper

Preheat oven to 425 degrees. Use either a food processor fitted with a plastic blade, or a mixing bowl and a wooden spoon to blend all ingredients together until a smooth dough is formed. Roll dough into cherry-sized balls and place on ungreased baking sheet and bake for 6–10 minutes. Serve immediately. **Makes approximately 18 cheese bites.**

Tuna Pâté

Another treat from my "sounds gross, tastes great" collection. If you're thinking pâté is passé, you may want to think again—this recipe is always a hit.

2 cans solid white albacore tuna, packed in oil, drained and flaked
1 (8-oz) package cream cheese, room temperature
2 tbsp Heinz® Chili Sauce
2 tbsp fresh parsley, chopped
1 tsp dried minced onion
¼ tsp Tabasco® Sauce

Using a food processor, pulse tuna and cream cheese together. Add all remaining ingredients, pulsing until well combined. Cover and chill for at least an hour. Bring to room temperature before serving. Serve with unseasoned small crackers or Melba Toasts. **Serves 8.**

Marinated Shrimp & Artichokes

The robust chive and parsley marinade used to flavor this appetizer can also be used as a dressing—it's delicious tossed with garden greens or drizzled over freshly steamed and chilled asparagus.

24 whole cooked shrimp, tails removed

2 (14-oz) cans artichoke bottoms,
     drained and sliced into strips

1 large whole egg yolk

½ cup extra-virgin olive oil

½ cup vegetable oil

¼ cup red wine vinegar

2 tbsp Dijon mustard

2 tbsp fresh scallions, minced

2 tbsp fresh parsley, chopped

2 tbsp fresh chives, chopped

½ tsp salt

½ tsp granulated sugar

Black pepper, freshly ground

Place prepared shrimp and artichokes in a medium bowl and set aside. In a blender, combine the egg yolk, oils, vinegar, mustard, scallions, parsley, chives, salt, sugar and black pepper. Whirl until well blended. Pour marinade over shrimp and artichokes and toss to coat. Cover and refrigerate for at least 6 hours prior to serving. **Serves 12.**

Roasted Rack of Lamb

2 to 3 racks of lamb rib chops, French-trimmed

HERB PASTE:
2 cups fresh mint leaves
2 fresh rosemary sprigs, leaves only
2 tbsp fresh parsley
2 garlic cloves
¼ tsp salt
¼ tsp black pepper, freshly ground
2–3 tbsp extra-virgin olive oil
4 tbsp unsalted butter, melted
1 cup homemade breadcrumbs (recipe follows)

Have your butcher "French trim" the lamb rib chops (removal of the bone that attaches the chops will allow for easier cutting of individual chops once cooked).

Preheat oven to 500 degrees. Cover exposed bones with foil to keep from burning. In the bowl of a food processor, combine the mint leaves, rosemary, parsley, garlic, salt and pepper. Pulse until finely chopped. Add the olive oil one tablespoon at a time in a steady stream until mixture comes together to form a chunky paste.

Lightly cover lamb with herb paste. Place lamb racks on slotted roasting or broiling pan and roast for 10 minutes. Remove from oven and reduce heat to 400 degrees. In a small bowl, toss 2 tablespoons of the melted butter with the breadcrumbs. Lightly sprinkle mixture over tops of lamb and then drizzle with remaining 2 tablespoons of butter. Return lamb racks to the oven and roast for an additional 10–15 minutes. Lamb should be pink on the inside (not rare). Cut lamb racks into individual chops before serving. **Serves 8–10.**

Homemade Breadcrumbs

Homemade breadcrumbs—who has the time? For a memorable meal like this one, YOU DO. It's so worth it.

6 slices white bread, several days old

Preheat oven to 250 degrees. Lay bread slices in a single layer on an ungreased baking sheet and dry in oven until crisp, but not brown. Cool bread completely. Place in food processor and pulse until bread crumbs are coarse. Alternately, bread may be placed in a paper bag and crushed with a rolling pin. Crumbs may be stored in a tightly sealed container for up to a week.
Makes approximately 1 cup.

Broiled Salmon

6 (8-oz) center-cut, skin-on pieces of fresh salmon filet, bones removed
Lawry's® Seasoned Salt or Lemon Pepper Seasoning, to taste
Paprika, to taste
2 lemons, cut into wedges
¼ cup fresh dill, chopped
3 tbsp unsalted butter
Tangy Tartar Sauce (recipe follows)

Move oven rack to middle position and turn oven to broil setting. Wash salmon pieces and pat dry with paper towel. Lightly grease a flat Pyrex baking dish and lay salmon skin-side down. Season filets with seasoned salt or lemon pepper seasoning and paprika. Squeeze 1 lemon wedge over each piece. Sprinkle with fresh dill and dot each piece of fish with ½ tablespoon of butter. Broil salmon on middle rack of oven for 10 minutes, then reduce heat to 350 degrees and bake another 10–12 minutes, depending on the thickness of the filet, until fish is just cooked through. Serve with tangy tartar sauce (recipe follows). **Serves 6.**

Tangy Tartar Sauce

Homemade tartar sauce makes such a difference! This fresh, easy recipe is not only delicious with broiled salmon, but works well with a variety of seafoods.

2 tsp dill pickle, chopped
2 tsp sweet pickle, chopped
2 tsp fresh yellow onion, grated
1 green olive, chopped
1 black olive, chopped
1 garlic clove, minced
10 sprigs fresh parsley, very finely chopped
1 cup mayonnaise
1 ½ tbsp lemon juice, freshly squeezed
1 tsp prepared horseradish, drained

Combine pickles, onion, olives, garlic and parsley and then chop everything once again. In a small bowl, mix together mayonnaise, lemon juice and horseradish. Add mayonnaise mixture by heaping spoonfuls to chopped mixture until desired consistency is reached. **Makes 1 ½ cups.**

Green Bean Purée

1 lb fresh green beans or haricots verts
4 tbsp unsalted butter
4 tbsp heavy cream
Kosher salt, to taste
Black pepper, freshly ground to taste

Trim ends of beans and cook until crisp tender. Drain well. While beans are still hot, place in a blender and add the butter. Let the butter begin to melt on the warm beans. Add 2 tablespoons of the cream and whir in blender on high for 20 seconds. Add remaining cream 1 tablespoon at a time and continue to blend on high until desired consistency. Purée should be smooth and thick—not watery. Season with salt and pepper to taste. **Serves 8.**

Cauliflower Purée

For some reason, purée in America is relegated to one of three categories: mashed potatoes, applesauce or baby food. But I prefer to think of it from a more French POV: it's an opportunity to take something perfectly healthy and sully it in the best way—with butter, cream and salt. The French invented purée, after all. Along with croissants and fondue. So it's possible that their culinary instincts can be trusted.

2 lb fresh cauliflower, washed, dried and cut into small florets
2–3 tbsp half & half or whole milk
½ cup Parmigiano-Reggiano cheese, freshly grated

½ tsp kosher salt
Black pepper, freshly ground to taste
¼ tsp garlic powder
¼ tsp onion powder

Place cauliflower in microwave-safe baking dish and cover with ¼ cup of water. Cover dish completely with plastic wrap, and poke holes in the plastic so that steam can escape. Microwave on high for 3 minutes, until cauliflower is very soft. Use a slotted spoon to remove cauliflower from baking dish and place in a blender or food processor. Whir or pulse cauliflower for 20 seconds. Add half & half and cheese and continue to blend for another 30 seconds. Add salt, pepper, garlic powder and onion powder and blend again until just combined. Adjust seasonings and add additional half & half only as needed. Purée should have the consistency of mashed potatoes. **Serves 8.**

Mustard Roasted Potatoes

2 lb baby potatoes, Yukon gold or baby red
½ cup mayonnaise
2 tbsp whole-grain mustard
2 tbsp Dijon mustard
2 garlic cloves, freshly pressed

1 tsp paprika
½ tsp ground cumin
½ tsp salt, plus more to taste
Black pepper, freshly ground to taste
2 tbsp fresh parsley, chopped

Wash and dry potatoes and set aside. In a medium bowl, combine mayonnaise, mustards, garlic, spices, salt and pepper. Whisk to blend. Cover and refrigerate for several hours. Preheat oven to 400 degrees. Lightly grease a roasting pan. Using a fork, prick potatoes all over several times. Toss potatoes with mustard/mayonnaise mixture, being sure to coat evenly. Pour coated potatoes into prepared pan and spread into a single layer. Bake for about 45 minutes until potatoes are fork-tender. Garnish with fresh parsley and salt. **Serves 8–10.**

Thelma's Old-Fashioned Birthday Cake

My mother was going through her own recipe box and found this long-lost treasure in family friend Thelma's own handwriting! Full disclosure: this recipe won't deliver the springy, ultra-moist texture you might expect from a boxcake—but it is delicious in its own crumbly way, and it's still our go-to birthday cake.

3 cups sifted cake flour (sift once before measuring, and again with dry ingredients)
3 ½ tsp baking powder
¼ tsp salt
1 ½ cups granulated sugar
¾ cup unsalted butter
2 tsp pure vanilla extract
5 large egg yolks
1 ¼ cup whole milk
Thelma's Fudge Frosting (recipe follows)

Preheat oven to 350 degrees. Grease and flour two deep 9-inch round aluminum cake pans. In a medium bowl, sift together flour, baking powder and salt—set aside. Using an electric mixer, cream the sugar and butter together. Scrape down sides of bowl to thoroughly mix. Add vanilla and egg yolks one at a time and continue mixing until smooth. Add flour mixture alternately with milk, scraping bowl while beating. Beat only enough to blend. Pour batter into prepared pans. Bake for 20–30 minutes until cake tops are golden brown and a cake tester inserted in the middle comes out clean. Let cool completely before removing from pans. Frost with Thelma's Fudge Frosting. **Serves 10—12.**

Thelma's Fudge Frosting

1 ¼ cups granulated sugar
1 cup heavy cream
5 oz unsweetened chocolate
½ cup unsalted butter
1 tsp pure vanilla extract

In a heavy saucepan, combine sugar and cream. Bring to a boil, stirring constantly. Reduce heat and simmer for 6 minutes without stirring. Remove from heat, add chocolate and stir until all of the chocolate has melted. Stir in butter and vanilla until it reaches a smooth consistency. Chill uncovered in refrigerator until mixture begins to thicken. Using an electric mixer, beat frosting until thick and creamy. Makes any cake more elegant and delicious! **Frosts 1 (9-inch) layer cake.**

Frozen Lemon Torte

Is there anyone who can't appreciate the glory of a torte? Hopefully you can—and using lady fingers makes this (or any) dessert more impressive.

2 (3-oz) packages soft lady fingers
3 large eggs, divided
1 cup granulated sugar, divided
1 ½ tbsp lemon zest

¼ cup lemon juice, freshly squeezed
2 tbsp cold water
1 cup heavy cream, whipped

Prepare an 8-inch springform pan by lining the interior rim with lady finger halves standing upright and with split sides facing inward. It's easiest to keep lady fingers attached as sheets and bend them to fit. You will need about 20 lady fingers to completely line the rim. Use additional lady fingers to line the bottom of the pan, being sure to cover completely. You will need to break some of them into smaller pieces to get a tight fit.

In a medium bowl, whisk egg yolks until thick and lemon-colored. Add ½ cup sugar, lemon zest, lemon juice and water. Whisk until smooth. Place mixture in the top of a double boiler and cook over rapidly boiling water until thickened—about 10 minutes. Remove from heat and cool completely. Meanwhile beat egg whites with an electric mixer, gradually adding the remaining ½ cup of sugar until glossy and stiff. Fold lemon custard mixture into beaten egg whites. Fold in whipped cream and pour mixture into prepared pan, using a spatula to smooth top. Cover and freeze at least 6 hours or overnight. Remove from freezer 10 minutes before serving. **Serves 10.**

This whimsical Argenta stoneware was crafted in Stockholm during the Art Deco period. The pieces are first glazed, then hand-painted with silver overlay in fantastical shapes: mermaids and other mythical sea creatures, majestic lions and more. It's one of our most interesting collections—always inviting discussion and evoking delight.

Fresh Strawberry Pie

This recipe was my Aunt Joanie's take on fresh strawberries and cream—light, fruity and just delightful. It can be made with a graham cracker crust as well. Either way, just be sure to serve shortly after making, as the glazed pie doesn't hold for more than a few hours in the refrigerator.

1 (9-inch) pre-baked pie shell (see Thelma's Pie Crust recipe on page 165)
6 oz cream cheese, room temperature
2 tsp pure vanilla extract
1 cup confectioner's sugar
2 cups heavy cream, whipped
3 cups fresh strawberries, small size
1 (12-oz) jar red currant jelly, melted and cooled

In a medium bowl, use an electric mixer to beat together the cream cheese, vanilla and sugar. Set aside. In a separate small bowl, beat the heavy cream until firm. Fold whipped cream into cream cheese mixture until just combined. Use a spatula to spread filling into prepared pie shell and smooth top. Cover and refrigerate for at least 4 hours or until filling is very firm.

Pick over berries to find ones that are all approximately the same small size—don't be tempted to use large berries, as these will be difficult to cut through when slicing the pie. Wash and dry selected strawberries. Slice off tops so that berries will sit flat on top of pie, pointed side up. Once pie filling is completely chilled, arrange strawberries tightly together on top of pie so that none of the filling shows. Spoon currant jelly over strawberries until the top is fully glazed. Refrigerate before serving. **Serves 8.**

The unusual glazed plates pictured here were hand-painted by early 20th-century artist and ceramist Edith Varian Cockcroft—a precocious young American who traveled to France in 1898, at age 17, to study art with Henri Matisse. I discovered them online and fell instantly in love.

Celebrate Summer

The summers of my childhood were defined by long, drowsy days at the lake and illuminated by lightning storms and legions of fireflies—our cocktail of choice was water, drunk straight from the hose. But regardless of where one might have been raised, summer brings with it a thrilling sense of freedom that everyone, everywhere, can enjoy.

This menu is meant to capture that feeling, and is therefore best enjoyed outdoors, in the company of good friends. Wherever possible, I have used fruits and vegetables that are widely in season—but if something comparable is available where you live, by all means use your local produce instead!

Refreshment
Watermelon Agua Fresca

Starters
Gazpacho Soup Shots

Spicy Parmesan Kale Chips

Crudités with Barb's Best Dip

Mediterranean Quinoa Salad

Corn off the Cob Salad

Classic Caesar Salad

On the Grill
Beef Tenderloin Kabobs

Swordfish Kabobs

Sweets
Peach Cobbler

Olallieberrie Pie

Mom's Best-Ever Cheesecake

Watermelon Agua Fresca

Traditional Mexican aguas frescas are made with added sugar—to which I'm obviously not opposed—but this recipe is perfectly summery and sweet just the way it is. The only way I've found to improve it is to add copious amounts of liquor.

1 small ripe seedless watermelon
Juice from 4 limes, freshly squeezed
Fresh mint, for garnish

Slice watermelon and remove rind. Cut watermelon flesh into small chunks sized to easily fit through an electric juicer. Juice watermelon chunks and pour liquid though a fine mesh strainer to remove pulp. Pour watermelon juice into a large pitcher. Add freshly squeezed lime juice to taste. Serve over ice and garnish with fresh mint. **Serves 8.**

Gazpacho Soup Shots

3 medium ripe tomatoes, peeled,
seeded and diced

3 cups tomato juice

¼ cup Vidalia onion, diced

½ fresh green bell pepper, seeded and diced

¼ cup fresh yellow or orange bell peppers

½ fresh red bell pepper, seeded and diced

¼ cup green onions, chopped

2 tbsp fresh parsley, chopped

1 tbsp fresh dill, chopped

1 fresh English cucumber, peeled and chopped

3 garlic cloves, minced

1 tsp Worcestershire sauce

3 tbsp red wine vinegar

½ tsp Tabasco Sauce, or more to taste

½ tsp Maggi® Liquid Seasoning, or more to taste

½ tsp ground cumin

⅛ tsp black pepper, freshly ground

Mix all ingredients together and pulse through a food processor or blender to desired consistency. Place in large glass bowl, cover and chill at least 8 hours or overnight to blend flavors before serving. **Makes 30 soup shots.**

Spicy Parmesan Kale Chips

Like bacon, cheese makes everything—even kale—taste delicious!

1 large bunch fresh Lacinato kale
Extra-virgin olive oil spray (I use a Misto sprayer)
Cayenne pepper, to taste
½ cup Parmigiano-Reggiano cheese, freshly grated

Preheat oven to 300 degrees. Wash kale leaves very well with cold water and pat each leaf dry with paper towel. Cut away leaves from thick center rib. Discard rib. Place leaves dark side up in a single layer but very close together on an ungreased baking sheet. Lightly spray leaves with oil, sprinkle with cayenne pepper and cheese. Bake 18–20 minutes until leaves begin to crisp and cheese starts to slightly brown. Serve warm or at room temperature. These keep well in an airtight container for up to a week. **Serves 4–6.**

Crudités with Barb's Best Dip

This recipe, originally shared by family friend Barb, has been a summer staple of ours for more than 35 years. I have literally never served this dip without someone asking for the recipe. It's remarkably easy, absolutely everybody loves it, and best of all, it's NOT ranch dressing!

1 cup mayonnaise
2 tbsp ketchup
1 ½ tbsp yellow onion, coarsely grated
2 tsp tarragon vinegar
¼ tsp dried thyme
¼ tsp curry powder
¼ tsp salt
Assorted fresh vegetables, for dipping

In a small bowl, mix all ingredients together with spatula. Cover and refrigerate overnight to blend flavors. Serve with a variety of fresh, seasonal vegetables. Dip will keep in airtight container in refrigerator for up to two weeks—but it probably won't last that long! **Makes 1 cup.**

Mediterranean Quinoa Salad

FOR THE DRESSING:
2 tbsp red wine vinegar
1 tbsp lemon juice, freshly squeezed
1 clove garlic, pressed
1 tsp dried oregano
3 tbsp extra-virgin olive oil
Salt, to taste
Black pepper, freshly ground to taste

FOR THE SALAD:
1 cup quinoa, uncooked
1 ¾ cups water
1 cup fresh red and yellow grape tomatoes, cut in half lengthwise
½ cup fresh English cucumber, sliced into rounds
        and then cut in half
½ cup Kalamata olives, pitted and sliced in half lengthwise
⅓ cup feta cheese, crumbled (I prefer French feta)
¼ cup sweet red onion, sliced into thin strip

In a small bowl, whisk together vinegar, lemon juice, garlic and dried oregano. Add olive oil and whisk until emulsified. Season with salt and pepper. Set aside.

Place uncooked quinoa in a fine mesh strainer and rinse well with cold water. Shake out excess water and place quinoa in a medium sauce pot. Add 1 ¾ cups of water, bring to a vigorous boil, and then reduce heat to simmer. Cover pot and continue to simmer for 15 minutes, until all of the liquid is absorbed. Remove from heat, fluff with a fork and transfer cooked quinoa to a large mixing bowl and allow to cool. You will have about 3 cups of cooked quinoa.

Add the tomatoes, cucumber, olives, cheese and onions to the cooled quinoa. Toss with a spatula to combine. Drizzle dressing 1 tablespoon at a time over quinoa, using only enough to coat. Cover and refrigerate quinoa salad until ready to serve. **Serves 6–8.**

Corn off the Cob Salad

6 whole ears of fresh sweet corn, husks removed and rinsed clean
2 tbsp unsalted butter
1 tbsp fresh thyme leaves, finely chopped
Lawry's Lemon Pepper Seasoning, to taste
Fresh chive blossoms, for garnish

Place corn in large pot and fill with cold water so that all of the cobs are submerged. Bring water to a hard boil and then immediately turn off heat. Let corn sit uncovered for a few minutes until it's cool enough to handle, but still warm. Remove from water and drain well. Use a sharp knife to cut kernels off of the cob. Place warm kernels in a medium bowl, add the butter and toss until melted. Add thyme and seasoning to taste. Garnish with fresh chive blossoms. **Serves 8–10.**

Classic Caesar Salad

FOR THE DRESSING:
¾ cup vegetable oil
¾ cup extra-virgin olive oil
¼ cup lemon juice, freshly squeezed
2 tbsp fresh garlic, pressed
2 tbsp whole-grain mustard
2 tbsp red wine vinegar
2 tbsp mayonnaise
2 tbsp Worcestershire sauce
1 tbsp anchovy paste
1 tbsp wasabi horseradish cream
      (Inglehoffer makes a good blend)
1 tsp black pepper, freshly ground
Salt, to taste

FOR THE CROUTONS:
2 ¼ cups baguette bread, cut into
      ¾ inch cubes
2 ½ tbsp extra-virgin olive oil
1 tbsp hot chili oil
¼ tsp salt
2 tbsp Parmigiano-Reggiano cheese,
      freshly grated

FOR THE SALAD:
3 hearts of Romaine, torn
Caesar dressing
Homemade croutons
½ cup Parmigiano-Reggiano cheese,
      freshly grated

For the dressing: In a medium bowl, whisk all ingredients together except for oils. Slowly add oils in steady stream while rapidly whisking until emulsified. Refrigerate at least one day before serving to allow flavors to blend.

For the croutons: In a medium sauté pan, add the oils and salt and heat over medium flame until very warm. Add the bread cubes and toss well to coat evenly. Continue stirring bread cubes while they cook—they should become nicely browned and crisp in a few minutes, so watch closely to avoid burning.

Place the warm croutons in brown paper bag, close the top and shake for a minute or so, allowing the paper to absorb the excess oil. Pour croutons into a second clean brown paper bag, add the cheese, close the bag and shake again for another minute to coat. Place finished croutons in a bowl until ready to use.

Place torn pieces of lettuce in a large bowl. Drizzle dressing ¼ cup at a time over salad using only enough to lightly coat the leaves. Gently toss and drizzle again as needed. Add croutons and sprinkle with cheese and a generous amount of coarsely ground black pepper. **Serves 12.**

Beef Tenderloin Kabobs

These flavorful kabobs are always a hit, and they are delicious served cold the next day, too.

FOR MARINADE:
¾ cup soy sauce
1 ½ cups vegetable oil
¼ cup Worcestershire sauce
2 tbsp dry mustard
1 ½ tsp fresh parsley
1 tbsp black pepper, coarsely ground
½ cup red wine vinegar
1 garlic clove, crushed
½ cup lemon juice, freshly squeezed

FOR KABOBS:
2 lb prime center-cut filet of beef, cut into 2-inch cubes
1 each red, green, yellow and orange bell peppers, stems removed, seeded and cut into 2-inch squares
2 sweet red onions, cut into 2-inch squares
1 cup fresh cherry tomatoes
12 whole white button mushroom caps, cleaned, stems removed

In a blender, whir all marinade ingredients together until frothy. Place beef and vegetables in separate large glass bowls. Add ¾ of the marinade to the beef, toss to coat well, cover and refrigerate overnight. Use the remaining ¼ of the marinade and add to vegetables, toss to coat well, cover and refrigerate overnight. To assemble kabobs, spear beef, peppers, onions, tomatoes and mushroom caps on skewers, alternating between meat and vegetables. Broil or grill until brown on one side, then turn over and brown the other side. **Serves 8.**

Swordfish Kabobs

FOR MARINADE:
½ cup unsweetened pineapple juice
Juice of 3 limes, freshly squeezed, plus a bit of lime peel
1 tbsp fresh dill, chopped
¼ cup soy sauce, for brushing

FOR KABOBS:
2 lb fresh swordfish, cut into 2-inch cubes
2 Vidalia onions, cut into wedges
3 limes, cut into thin slices
1 cup fresh pineapple chunks

In a large bowl, combine pineapple juice, lime juice, lime peel and dill. Add swordfish and toss to coat. Marinate for 20 minutes—be sure not to let fish sit for too long, as the lime juice will begin to cook the fish. To assemble kabobs, spear swordfish, pineapple, onion and lime slices with skewers, alternating between fish and fruit. Brush kabobs with soy sauce. Broil or grill for 10–15 minutes, turning a few times to cook evenly on all sides. **Serves 8.**

Peach Cobbler

FOR FILLING:

10 ripe peaches, pitted, peeled and sliced

4 tbsp granulated sugar

Juice of 1 lemon, freshly squeezed

1 whole soft vanilla bean

FOR TOPPING:

1 ½ cups self-rising flour, unleveled

¼ cup granulated sugar

¼ tsp salt

6 tbsp unsalted butter

½ cup buttermilk

2 tbsp turbinado sugar, for sprinkling on top

Preheat oven to 425 degrees. In medium bowl, combine peaches, sugar and lemon juice. Split vanilla bean in half and scrape seeds into bowl with peaches. Gently toss and macerate mixture for 10 minutes. Place mixture in an ungreased shallow 8-inch square glass or ceramic baking dish. Bake peaches for approximately 20 minutes, or until they start to become soft and juicy. Remove peaches from oven and reduce oven temperature to 375 degrees.

Make the biscuit topping by combining flour, sugar and salt in a medium bowl. Cut in butter until a coarse crumb forms. Add buttermilk and mix gently until biscuit dough forms. Take small scoops of dough and pat them down between the palms of your hands to form flat disks. Place biscuit disks randomly over pre-baked peaches, leaving some areas of fruit exposed. Sprinkle with turbinado sugar and return to oven. Bake for another 30 minutes or until biscuit topping is golden brown.
Serves 6–8.

Olallieberry Pie

Never heard of an olallieberry? That's because they're grown almost exclusively in the areas surrounding the quaint coastal town of Cambria, California. I believe their complex berry flavor is perfect for a summer pie, but if you can't find them, fear not! Blackberries, boysenberries, raspberries (or any combination of the three) will work equally well.

1 (10-inch) unbaked pie crust (see Thelma's
    Pie Crust recipe on page 165)

4 cups fresh olallieberries

1 cup granulated sugar

4 tbsp cornstarch

1 tbsp lemon juice, freshly squeezed

1 tsp lemon zest

⅓ cup crème de cassis or blackberry liqueur

Pinch salt

2 tbsp unsalted butter, cut into pieces

Preheat oven to 425 degrees. Make pie crust according to Thelma's recipe for 10-inch pie. Use ¾ of the dough to make a 9-inch pie crust and reserve ¼ of dough to make lattice top. In a medium bowl, toss olallieberries together with sugar. In a separate small bowl, whisk together cornstarch, lemon juice, lemon zest, crème de cassis and salt. Gently combine liquid mixture with berries and toss until coated. Place berry mixture into prepared pie crust and dot with butter. Roll out remaining dough and use a fluted-edge pastry cutter to cut even-width strips, approximately one-inch wide. Place strips over berries and weave into lattice pattern. Place pie on rimmed baking sheet and bake for 15 minutes. Reduce heat to 350 degrees and bake for another 30–40 minutes until crust is golden brown and berry filling is bubbling. **Serves 8.**

Mom's Best-Ever Cheesecake

FOR CRUST:

1 ⅓ cups Nilla Wafers® crumbs

⅓ cup butter or margarine, melted

⅓ cup granulated sugar

1 tsp ground cinnamon

FOR FILLING:

5 (8-oz) packages cream cheese, room temperature

1 ¾ cups granulated sugar

3 tbsp all-purpose flour

1 tsp lemon zest

1 tsp orange zest

¼ tsp salt

½ tsp pure vanilla extract

5 large eggs, room temperature

2 large egg yolks, room temperature

¼ cup heavy cream

Preheat oven to 500 degrees. In a medium bowl, make the crust by combining wafer crumbs, butter or margarine, sugar and cinnamon and mix well. Press into bottom and slightly up the sides of 9-inch springform pan, cover and chill in the refrigerator.

Meanwhile, make the filling by using an electric mixer to beat cream cheese and sugar together until light and fluffy. Add flour, lemon zest, orange zest, salt and vanilla and continue to beat. Add eggs one at a time followed by egg yolks one at a time, beating well after each addition. With a spatula, gently stir in the cream by hand. Pour into prepared crust and bake at 500 degrees for 10 minutes. Without opening oven door, turn oven temperature down to 200 degrees and bake for 1 more hour. Turn off heat and leave cheesecake in closed oven for 2 more hours, or until completely cooled. Remove from oven and let stand at room temperature for 15 minutes. Remove sides from springform pan and cover cheesecake with plastic wrap. Chill in refrigerator overnight before serving. **Serves 12–14.**

The mosaic pieces in this chapter come from the early 20th-century French tradition of pique assiette, which literally means "he who eats from another's plate." Each item is delightfully different—and together, they grace our table with a sense of shared history that's ideal for a buffet-style gathering.

La Dolce Vita

I cannot imagine any place more romantic than Italy's Amalfi Coast; it really is like walking into a breathtaking daydream. This menu is meant to evoke the feeling of a lazy afternoon in this incomparable Mediterranean paradise, with absolutely nothing to do but soak one's palate in sunny flavors and drowse in the dappled sunlight.

Although it certainly doesn't hurt for one to actually BE in coastal Italy, I like to think that the concept of la dolce vita—the sweet life—is a state of mind. The trick is to completely surrender oneself to the simple flavors of a life lived to its absolute fullest. If even for a few hours, I hope this menu helps you do just that.

Libation
Jimmy's Homemade Limoncello

Starters
Zucchini Fries with Spicy Roasted Red Pepper
     Dipping Sauce
Chilled Cantaloupe Soup with Crispy Prosciutto
Heirloom Tomato Bruschetta

Savories
Chopped Antipasto Salad
    Three-Week Vinaigrette Dressing
    Quick Vinaigrette Dressing
Spaghetti Cacio e Pepe
Penne Bolognese
Bell Peppers Stuffed with Spicy Italian Sausage
Dominick's Mom's Eggplant Parmigiana
Grilled Chicken Breasts with Lemon & Herbs

Sweets
Grandma Dorothy's Faux-Cotta
    Cheesecake
Fresh Mixed Berry Tart
Assorted Cookies:
    Italian Wedding
    Classic Anisette
    Pine Nut
Chocolate Lattice Tart

Jimmy's Homemade Limoncello

This tangy, traditional limoncello recipe was crafted by our colorful family friend, Jimmy "The Fur," who—not surprisingly—has substantial roots in Italy. It's delicious when made with all lemons or with a few orange peels thrown in for additional depth of flavor. Just don't be tempted to taste as you go, as the combination of grain alcohol and peeling knives is unlikely to make your preparations unfold as planned.

½ **gallon grain alcohol (I use Everclear) or unflavored 100-proof vodka**
30 lemons
¾ **gallon water**
4–5 cups granulated sugar

Pour alcohol into a large bowl or glass jar with a lid. Use a vegetable peeler or very sharp paring knife to carefully peel only the top layer of skin from the lemons into wide strips—no white pithy parts. Discard the fruit (or better yet, set aside to juice for lemonade, later). Place the peels into the container with the alcohol, cover with lid, and freeze for 2-4 weeks to infuse liquor with citrus oils.

After infusing, remove container from freezer and bring to room temperature. Remove peels and discard. In a large pot, bring ¾ gallon of water to a boil. Add 4–5 cups sugar, depending upon how sweet you prefer your limoncello. Stir until sugar is completely dissolved and liquid is clear. Remove pan from heat, and let sugar water cool. When mixture reaches room temperature, add to the lemon-infused alcohol. Presto! Limoncello! Serve ice-cold. **Makes approximately 1 ½ gallons.**

Zucchini Fries

Chef Fabrizio Giorgi from Café Sapori graciously shared this outstanding recipe for crispy fried zucchini and his signature dipping sauce—along with a few tips on getting the zucchini perfectly crispy.

10 fresh zucchini, sliced into thin strips
10 oz semolina flour
8 oz all-purpose flour
4 cups whole milk
3 large eggs
24 fl oz vegetable oil, for frying
1 bunch fresh basil leaves
1 bunch fresh parsley leaves (flat-leaf variety)
Salt, to taste

Use a mandoline to cut the zucchini into thin strips. NOTE: Use ONLY the part of the zucchini with the skin—the middle of the zucchini is too soft and will not get crispy when fried.

In a medium bowl, combine both flours together and set aside. In a separate large bowl, whisk together milk and eggs. Dip zucchini strips in liquid, shake off excess and dip into flour mixture. Shake off excess flour.

In a heavy pot, heat vegetable oil until temperature reaches 370 degrees on a candy thermometer. Fry small batches of zucchini strips until they begin to crisp and turn golden—approximately 3 minutes. Toss in basil and parsley leaves right at the end. Fry for an additional 30 seconds.

Remove with a slotted spoon and drain everything together on paper towels. Sprinkle zucchini strips with salt and garnish with crispy basil and parsley leaves. Serve immediately with a side of roasted red pepper dipping sauce (recipe follows). **Serves 10—12.**

Spicy Roasted Red Pepper Dipping Sauce

4 fresh tomatoes (I use Roma variety)
1 fresh red bell pepper
1 fresh jalapeño pepper
¼ cup fresh green onion, chopped
½ cup chicken or vegetable broth
½ tsp salt
1–2 tbsp extra-virgin olive oil

Place whole tomatoes, red pepper and jalapeño pepper on a very hot grill. Turn frequently until they are charred and blistering on all sides. Remove vegetables from grill, place peppers in a brown paper bag, fold top to seal and let sit for 15 minutes. Place tomatoes in a separate bowl, and when slightly cooled remove and discard tomato stems and skin. Cut tomato flesh into large chunks and place in a medium sauce pot.

Remove peppers from bag and gently remove skins. Cut peppers in half, remove stems and seeds and cut pepper flesh into chunks. Add all of the red pepper to sauce pot, but add only ¼–½ of the jalapeño pepper, depending upon how spicy you like your sauce. Add onion and stir to combine.

Add broth to pot and bring mixture to a boil, stirring constantly. Reduce heat to medium high and continue cooking until all of the liquid is absorbed and the tomatoes, peppers and onion are very soft—about 8 minutes. Remove pot from heat and let mixture cool to room temperature.

Place mixture in a blender and blend until chunky. Add oil and purée until sauce is smooth but still thick. Serve warm with zucchini fries. Sauce will keep well in the refrigerator for a week—just reheat before serving. **Makes approximately 1 cup.**

Chilled Cantaloupe Soup with Crispy Prosciutto

1 ripe cantaloupe, rind and seeds removed, flesh cut into small chunks
1 cup orange juice, freshly squeezed
½ cup plain yogurt
1 tbsp lime juice, freshly squeezed
8 slices imported prosciutto, for garnish
Fresh borage flowers, for garnish

In a blender, combine cantaloupe, orange juice, yogurt and lime juice. Blend until soup is very smooth. Cover and chill several hours in refrigerator. To make the crispy prosciutto, place thin slices of prosciutto in a large skillet and cook over medium heat until prosciutto becomes crispy. Drain well on paper towels and cool completely. Crumble prosciutto and store in an airtight container until ready to use. To serve, garnish chilled soup with crispy prosciutto and fresh borage flowers.
Serves 6.

Heirloom Tomato Bruschetta

1 loaf baguette bread

¼ cup extra-virgin olive oil, plus 1 tbsp

1 clove garlic, pressed

4 fresh heirloom tomatoes

2 tbsp fresh basil, chopped

2 tsp balsamic vinegar glaze

Salt, to taste

Black pepper, freshly ground to taste

Preheat oven to 375 degrees. Slice crusty baguette bread into 18 rounds—each approximately ½ inch thick. In a small bowl, combine oil and garlic. Use a pastry brush to lightly brush one side of the bread rounds with garlic infused oil. Place bread slices oiled side down on ungreased baking sheet. Bake for 12–15 minutes or until bread is lightly browned and crunchy.

Line a medium bowl with several layers of paper towel. This will help absorb the extra tomato juice and seeds. Cut the tomatoes into medium-size dice and place in prepared bowl. Let tomatoes sit for 5 minutes. Discard soaked paper towel, and return tomatoes to a clean, dry bowl. Add basil and gently toss. In a small bowl, whisk together reserved 1 tablespoon of oil with vinegar glaze and pour over tomato and basil mixture. Gently stir to combine. Season with salt and pepper to taste.

Use a slotted spoon to place tomato mixture on top of each baked bread slice. Sprinkle again with salt and pepper and serve immediately. **Makes 18 bruschetta.**

Chopped Antipasto Salad

2 small heads iceberg lettuce, washed and dried

1 cup Italian salami, sliced into thin strips

1 cup provolone cheese, cubed

1 cup fresh grape tomatoes, sliced in half

1 cup garbanzo beans, well drained

1 cup Kalamata olives, sliced in half

1 cup peperoncini, chopped

½ cup sweet red onion, thinly sliced

Chop lettuce into small chunks. Place in a large bowl. Add all remaining ingredients. Toss lightly with either of the vinaigrette dressings below. **Serves 8.**

Three-Week Vinaigrette Dressing

2 cups red wine vinegar

1 cup cider vinegar

1 tbsp granulated sugar

½ tsp salt

1 garlic clove, mashed

½ shallot, finely chopped

4 sprigs fresh parsley, finely chopped

1 sprig fresh dill, finely chopped

¼ stalk fresh celery, finely chopped

¼ tsp cayenne pepper

1 tsp Dijon mustard

1 ½ cups olive oil

1 ½ cups vegetable oil

Make the vinegar by combining all ingredients together EXCEPT OILS in a glass mason jar fitted loosely with a lid. Let steep for 3 weeks at room temperature. When mixture is steeped, strain through a fine cheesecloth, reserving clear infused vinegar.

For every 1 cup of seasoned vinegar, add 1 ½ cups of olive oil and 1 ½ cups vegetable oil. Add oils in steady stream until emulsified. The remainder of seasoned vinegar can be stored for later use. **Makes 6 cups.**

Quick Vinaigrette Dressing

¼ cup red wine vinegar

1 tsp Dijon mustard, heaping

1 garlic clove, minced

1 tbsp lemon juice, freshly squeezed

½ tsp salt

½ tsp black pepper, freshly ground

1 cup olive oil

In a medium bowl, whisk together vinegar, mustard and garlic. Add the lemon juice, salt and pepper. Slowly add the oil while mixing vigorously to emulsify. **Makes 1 ½ cups.**

Spaghetti Cacio e Pepe

The expression "don't mess with perfection" is aptly applied to this classic Italian preparation, in which three simple ingredients deliver truly exquisite flavor. Pasta, cheese and pepper—how could it be anything but perfect?

1 lb spaghetti pasta
2 cups Pecorino or Parmigiano-Reggiano cheese, freshly grated
2 tsp black pepper, coarsely ground

In a large pot, cook spaghetti in boiling water until al dente, about 10 minutes. Reserve ½ cup of the pasta water and discard the rest. Drain pasta and quickly return it to the same cooking pot while hot. Alternate adding grated cheese and reserved cooking water to pasta while stirring constantly, so that spaghetti becomes well coated with cheese. You may not need to use all of the water, only enough to help the cheese bind with the noodles. Sprinkle black pepper over pasta, one teaspoon at a time to taste. **Serves 6–8.**

Penne Bolognese

4 (28-oz) cans stewed tomatoes

2 (15-oz) cans tomato purée

2 yellow onions, chopped

2 tbsp of extra-virgin olive oil

4 lb ground beef chuck

Salt, to taste

Black pepper, freshly ground to taste

½ cup granulated sugar

¾ cup red or white wine

1 large bunch fresh parsley, chopped

1 tsp garlic, freshly pressed

2 dried bay leaves

1 ½ tsp dried basil

1 lb of penne noodles, cooked al dente

In a large pot, combine stewed tomatoes and tomato purée. In a separate sauté pan, cook the onion in oil until glossy and add to the tomatoes. Cook beef in the same sauté pan and season with salt and pepper. Leave the beef in large chunks and do not overcook it—brown only until the meat is no longer red. Drain fat, but reserve some of the juice. Add browned meat and juice to pot. Add sugar, wine, parsley, garlic, bay leaves and basil and stir well to combine. Add salt and pepper to taste. Cook over low heat, uncovered, for 1 ½–2 hours. Serve over cooked penne noodles. Extra sauce can be stored in the refrigerator for up to 1 week. **Serves 6–8.**

Bell Peppers Stuffed with Spicy Italian Sausage

2 lb spicy Italian sausage

1 yellow onion, finely chopped

1 lb fresh sliced mushrooms, finely chopped

¼ tsp crushed red pepper flakes

Maggi Liquid Seasoning, to taste

1 cup Parmigiano-Reggiano cheese,
    finely grated, plus extra for sprinkling

1 tbsp fresh oregano, finely chopped

½ cup unseasoned bread crumbs, scant

8 bell peppers—2 red, 2 yellow, 2 orange
      and 2 green

1 tbsp extra-virgin olive oil

Preheat oven to 375 degrees. Remove sausage filling from casings and discard casings. In a medium sauté pan, cook sausage over medium heat until it is thoroughly cooked but not too browned. Drain sausage on paper towels to absorb grease. Reserve 1 tablespoon of fat from pan, wipe pan clean and place reserved fat back in pan. Add onion and sauté until glossy—about 4 minutes. Add mushrooms and sauté together, stirring constantly, until mixture begins to change color. Add cooked sausage to mushroom/onion mixture and cook for another 5 minutes. Transfer mixture to a large mixing bowl and let cool for 10 minutes. Meanwhile, cut tops off of peppers and scoop out insides, removing ribs and seeds. Place peppers bottom side down in an ungreased 9x13 baking dish. Add cheese, oregano and breadcrumbs to the cooled sausage mixture and toss gently to combine.

Stuff peppers with sausage mixture and sprinkle each with extra teaspoon of cheese on top. Drizzle tops with oil. Bake for 30 minutes until tops are browned and crispy. **Makes 8 peppers.**

Dominick's Mom's Eggplant Parmigiana

A classic created by Dominick DiBartolomeo, whose delicious handcrafted specialty foods include fabulous pastas, sauces, tapenades and much more. Taste for yourself at www.domenicosfoods.com.

FOR THE MARINARA SAUCE:

2 (28-oz) cans San Marzano tomatoes (preferably D.O.P.), puréed in a blender

1 medium yellow onion, chopped

5 cloves of garlic, finely chopped

4 tbsp extra-virgin olive oil

Salt, to taste

FOR THE EGGPLANT:

6 large eggs

4 cups Italian seasoned breadcrumbs

3 medium eggplants, peeled and sliced about ⅛ inch thick

64 oz vegetable oil, for frying

2 cups of Parmigiano-Reggiano cheese, freshly grated

4 cups of whole-milk Mozzarella, shredded

FOR THE SAUCE: In a stockpot on medium-high heat, add the oil. Once the oil is hot, add the onion. Gently sauté until onion becomes tender and translucent, then add the garlic. Once the onions start to brown slightly, add the tomatoes. Reduce heat to low and allow the sauce to simmer uncovered for 30–45 minutes.

FOR THE EGGPLANT: In a medium mixing bowl, whisk together eggs until smooth and frothy. Place breadcrumbs in a large flat dish and evenly distribute. Dip the eggplant slices in the egg, then into the plate with the breadcrumbs to coat. Make sure the breadcrumbs completely cover the eggplant.

Preheat oven to 375 degrees. In a sauté pan on high heat, add the vegetable oil. Once the oil is hot enough, gently fry the prepared eggplant until golden brown. Remove and drain on paper towels. After all of the eggplant pieces are fried, ladle 8 oz of marinara sauce in a 9x13 baking dish and spread evenly to coat the bottom of the dish. Layer the bottom of the baking dish with eggplant, overlapping each piece. Once the bottom is covered, ladle another 8 oz of marinara sauce over the eggplant to completely cover it. Then generously sprinkle some of the mozzarella cheese over the eggplant. Finish off the layer by sprinkling a handful of grated Parmigiano-Reggiano cheese. Repeat the process to create two more layers of eggplant, sauce and cheese.

Cover the baking dish with aluminum foil and bake for 30 minutes or until all the cheese is melted. Uncover and bake for an additional 15–20 minutes, or until the top is golden brown. Remove from oven and allow to rest for 15 minutes before serving. **Serves 6–8.**

Grilled Chicken Breasts with Lemon & Herbs

8 whole skinless, boneless chicken breasts

¼ cup fresh garlic, finely chopped

½ cup rice vinegar

¼ cup water

¼ cup extra-virgin olive oil

¼ cup vegetable oil

2 tbsp dried oregano

2 tbsp dried rosemary

1 tbsp granulated sugar

1 tsp crushed red pepper flakes

1 large lemon, sliced thin

1 tsp black pepper, coarsely ground

1 tsp salt

Place chicken in a large glass bowl. In a separate bowl, make the marinade by combining all ingredients except salt and pepper. Mix well. Pour marinade over the chicken, cover and refrigerate for at least 4 hours. Remove chicken from marinade, leaving the herbs on, and season with salt and pepper. Cook chicken on very hot grill, turning a few times while cooking until chicken is done. Alternatively, the chicken may be broiled on a roasting pan in the oven for 8–10 minutes per side, or until it is cooked through. **Serves 8.**

Grandma Dorothy's Faux-Cotta Cheesecake

My husband always raved about his Grandma Dorothy's ricotta cheesecake. So when we finally got our hands on the recipe, I was shocked to learn that there isn't an ounce of ricotta in it! In the spirit of transparency, I've changed the name of this delicious, somewhat rustic treat to "faux-cotta."

1 (10-inch) springform pan filled with graham cracker crust (see recipe on page 168)

1 lb farmer's cheese, room temperature

3 large eggs, separated

1 cup granulated sugar, plus 1-2 tbsp

1 tsp pure vanilla extract

2 tsp lemon zest

½ cup whole milk, very scant

2 tbsp cornstarch

1 cup sour cream

Preheat oven to 325 degrees. Press graham cracker crust into the bottom of 10-inch springform pan. Cover and chill.

Use an electric mixer to beat together the cheese, egg yolks, 1 cup sugar, vanilla, lemon zest, milk, cornstarch and sour cream. Mix thoroughly until well combined. Set aside. Beat egg whites with 1-2 tablespoons of granulated sugar until stiff peaks form. Gently fold beaten egg whites into cheese mixture until just combined. Pour filling into prepared shell. Bake for 15 minutes, then reduce heat to 300 degrees and bake for another 45 minutes. Cool completely. Cover and chill in refrigerator for at least 8 hours before serving.

NOTE: Cheesecakes tend to leak liquid while cooking, so make sure to place a baking sheet lined with parchment paper or foil on the rack underneath your springform pan to prevent it from puddling on the bottom of your oven. **Serves 12.**

Fresh Mixed Berry Tart

This is a summery twist on the traditional Italian dessert, which typically pairs fresh fruit and heavy custard. Years ago, I started making a lighter version with fresh sweetened whipped cream and mixed seasonal berries— it became an instant family favorite, and I have made it this way ever since!

FOR FILLING:
1 (10-inch) pastry crust shell (recipe follows)
1 cup heavy cream
3 tbsp confectioner's sugar, heaping
1 tsp pure vanilla extract
2 ½ cups fresh mixed berries (I use a combination of raspberries, blueberries and blackberries)
Fresh edible flowers, for garnish

Use an electric mixer to whip together the cream, confectioner's sugar and vanilla extract until very firm. Use a spatula to spread sweetened whipped cream into prepared tart shell and smooth top. Refrigerate for at least 1 hour to allow filling to thoroughly chill and set. Before serving, randomly place berries over the filling, being mindful to leave some of the cream filling exposed around the edge. Garnish with fresh edible flowers. **Serves 10.**

Pastry Crust

1 cup unsalted butter, room temperature
½ cup granulated sugar
2 large egg yolks, well beaten
2 ½ cups all-purpose flour

½ tsp baking powder
1 tbsp lemon juice, freshly squeezed
1 tsp lemon zest

Preheat oven to 350 degrees. Grease a 10-inch removable bottom tart pan. Use an electric mixer to beat together the butter and sugar. Add egg yolks, scraping down sides of bowl to blend thoroughly. In a separate small bowl, sift together the flour and baking powder and add to the creamed mixture. Add lemon juice and lemon zest and continue scraping and mixing just until dough comes together. Do not over mix. Divide the dough in half and dump one portion in the center of prepared tart pan. Cover the other portion with plastic wrap and refrigerate for later use.

Using your fingertips, gently press dough into the bottom and up the sides of the prepared tart pan. Flatten dough in an even layer so that it has the same thickness throughout. Cover and refrigerate for 30 minutes. Prick crust all over with a fork. Bake for 10 minutes or just until crust begins to brown. Remove from oven and cool completely prior to filling. Reserved dough may be used to make an additional crust or cut into strips to create a lattice topping over baked fillings.
Makes 2 (10-inch) tart crusts.

Italian Wedding Cookies

Also known as Mexican Wedding Cookies or Viennese Crescents, these cookies have a light, nutty flavor that transcend ALL cultural divides.

1 cup unsalted butter, room temperature
¾ cup granulated sugar
1 cup raw nuts, ground (I use almonds)
2 ½ cups sifted all-purpose flour (sift before measuring)
¼ tsp salt
1 tsp pure vanilla extract
1 tsp pure almond extract
1 cup confectioner's sugar, sifted

Preheat oven to 350 degrees. In a medium bowl, use a wooden spoon to cream together butter and granulated sugar. Blend in nuts, flour, salt and extracts and stir until smooth. Let dough rest for a few minutes for easier handling. Shape into 1 ½-inch long crescents or balls. Bake on ungreased baking sheets for 10–13 minutes until lightly brown. Cool for 1 minute. While cookies are still warm, roll in or dust with confectioner's sugar and place on cooling rack until completely cool. Store in airtight container. **Makes 72 cookies.**

Classic Anisette Cookies

6 large eggs

8 tbsp butter or margarine, melted

2 tbsp vegetable oil

1 cup granulated sugar

1 tbsp anisette extract or pure vanilla extract

6 tsp baking powder

5-6 cups all-purpose flour

8 oz confectioner's sugar mixed with 2 tbsp of whole milk (optional)

½ cups confetti sprinkles (optional)

Preheat oven to 375 degrees. Use an electric mixer to beat the eggs until frothy. While eggs are beating, gradually add the butter or margarine, oil, granulated sugar and extract. Mix until well blended. Add baking powder and gradually add the flour, 1 cup at a time, mixing with your hands until you have a firm ball. Let dough rest for 10–15 minutes for easier handling.

Break off small pieces of dough and roll between your palms (like a pencil) to form a small tube; tie tube in a knot. You can also shape them into balls or rings. Bake on a greased cookie sheet for 12–15 minutes, or until golden brown.

NOTE: There are a number of variations on traditional anisette cookies, including those that are formed into biscotti-style loaves, sliced after baking and then lightly toasted again in the oven. Others are shaped in knots or balls, baked and then dipped in icing and sprinkled with confetti. They are delicious any way you make them. **Makes 36 cookies.**

Pine Nut Cookies

Adapted from the "Pignoli Cookies" recipe from King Arthur Flour Co., these delicious nut-crusted cookies are reminiscent of an almond macaroon.

1 cup almond paste

¼ cup granulated sugar

⅛ tsp salt

1 tsp pure almond extract

½ cup almond meal flour, finely ground

1 large egg white

1 ½ cups raw pine nuts

Preheat oven to 325 degrees. Line baking sheets with parchment paper. Use an electric mixer to blend together the almond paste, sugar, salt, almond extract and almond flour. Add the egg white and continue to blend until mixture is smooth. Place pine nuts in a shallow dish. Scoop 1-inch balls of dough into moist hands and drop dough balls into pine nuts. Roll around in the nuts until balls are completely covered. You may need to press them in slightly to get nuts to stick. Place on prepared baking sheets and bake for approximately 20 minutes, or until very lightly browned. Cool completely before serving. **Makes 24 cookies.**

Chocolate Lattice Tart

FOR THE PASTA FROLLA DOUGH:
1 ½ cups all-purpose flour
⅔ cup granulated sugar
2 tsp baking powder
2 large eggs
½ tsp pure vanilla extract
6 tbsp unsalted butter, melted
    and cooled

FOR THE FILLING:
4 oz unsweetened chocolate
8 tbsp unsalted butter
1 tbsp espresso powder
1 tbsp Grand Marnier®
4 large eggs
4 tsp light corn syrup
1 ¼ cups granulated sugar
¼ tsp salt
1 tsp pure vanilla extract
¼ cup whole milk, scant

FOR THE EGG WASH:
1 large egg mixed with
    1 tbsp water

FOR THE PASTA FROLLA DOUGH: In a large bowl, sift together the flour, sugar and baking powder. In a separate bowl, whisk together the eggs and vanilla until frothy. Pour egg mixture into dry ingredients and use a pastry cutter or fork to blend until crumbly. Pour melted butter over dough and mix until fully incorporated. The consistency will be wet and sticky. Let dough rest for 10 minutes for easier handling. Dump dough onto a well-floured board, sprinkle with additional flour and gently knead dough just until smooth. You will need to lightly sprinkle additional flour over dough a few times in order to handle, but use only as needed to keep it from sticking to your hands and to the board. Wrap dough in plastic wrap and refrigerate for at least 3 hours.

Preheat oven to 350 degrees. Lightly grease a 10-inch round shallow tart pan with a removable bottom. Divide the dough in half and return one portion to the refrigerator for later use. Gently press dough into tart shell and up sides of pan. Cover and refrigerate while preparing the filling.

FOR THE FILLING: In the top of a double boiler over medium heat, melt together chocolate and butter and stir until smooth. Set aside to cool. In a small bowl, dissolve espresso powder in Grand Marnier and add to chocolate mixture. Use an electric mixer to beat the eggs until frothy. Add corn syrup, sugar, salt, vanilla and milk. Beat well until mixture is thoroughly blended. Add chocolate mixture and continue to beat until just combined.

Pour filling into prepared tart crust, using only enough to fill the tart ¾ full (there will be leftover filling). Remove remaining portion of dough from refrigerator and roll out on a lightly floured board. Use a pastry cutter with a fluted edge to cut ¾-inch strips. Arrange strips in lattice pattern over top of filling. Trim excess dough from edges and gently brush or spray with egg wash. Place tart on rimmed baking sheet and bake for 30 minutes. Cool completely before serving. **Serves 10—12.**

Pizza Party with Chef Louise

For years, Chef Louise Leonard has been transforming a simple at-home pizza night into a raucous, unpredictable outdoor *fèsta* to which everyone wants an invitation. Louise's fresh, unexpected Neapolitan-style pies somehow elevate this simplest of dishes—delicious dough, secret sauces, surprising combinations—without changing its casual attitude.

Ingredients are sourced from the numerous farmers markets here in Los Angeles; everything is made from scratch, then charred to mouth-watering perfection. We always host this evening outside; if it's a bit chilly, that's just one more reason for us to gather around the wood-fired oven with our cocktails to watch Louise work her magic.

Summer Punch
Cucumber Mint Limeade

Nibbles
Roasted Almonds & Garbanzo Beans
Grilled Prosciutto-Wrapped Asparagus

Salad
Market Salad with Herbed Vinaigrette

Louise's Basics
Basic Pizza Dough
Classic Red Sauce
Classic Pesto Sauce

Pizzas
Margherita Pizza
Heirloom Tomatoes & Pesto Pizza
Sausage, Crispy Fennel & Sage Pizza
Broccolini, Mushroom & Fontina Pizza
Brie, Truffle Oil, Honey & Sea Salt Pizza
Hot Soppressata, Pepper, Onion &
     Pepperoncini Pizza

Desserts
Blueberry Crisp with
     Almond Streusel
Strawberry Ice Cream
Vanilla Bean Ice Cream
Luscious Lemon Ice Cream
Ferne Dickey's Ginger Snaps
Butter Crisp Sugar Cookies

Cucumber Mint Limeade

This limeade is the ultimate summer punch—it's easy to make, looks gorgeous on the table and is loved equally by children and adults. Our grown-up version is seasoned to taste with vodka, but liberal amounts of any clear spirit will do.

2 quarts (64 oz) pre-made limeade (I use Trader Joe's)
1 large lemon, microplaned for zest
4 fresh cucumbers, plus extra for garnish
1 bunch fresh mint leaves
Vodka or clear liquor of choice, to taste (optional)

Pour limeade into a large pitcher. Add the lemon zest. Use an electric juicer to collect 3 cups of cucumber juice. Add juice to limeade mixture and stir well. Crush a few mint sprigs to release flavor, and add to pitcher. Let steep for an hour in the refrigerator until the flavors have married. Serve over ice and garnish with a thin slice of cucumber and a sprig of mint. If using alcohol, pour liquor over ice first and then add limeade. **Serves 10.**

Roasted Almonds & Garbanzo Beans

Zest of 1 lemon
1 tbsp smoked paprika
1 tbsp garlic powder
1 tsp cayenne pepper
1 tbsp granulated sugar

Salt, to taste
1 cup extra-virgin olive oil
2 sprigs fresh rosemary
2 cups Marcona almonds
2 (15-oz) cans garbanzo beans, well drained

In a bowl, combine the lemon zest, paprika, garlic powder, cayenne pepper, sugar and salt, and set aside. Next, line a sheet pan with paper towels and set aside. Heat the oil in a wide sauté pan over medium-high heat to approximately 350 degrees. Add the rosemary until it just blisters—about 30 seconds. Remove with a slotted spoon and set on the prepared sheet pan. Next, fry the almonds until golden brown, about 2 minutes. Remove with a slotted spoon and add to the sheet pan. Sprinkle the almonds with half of the spice mixture. Finally, fry the garbanzos until crispy and golden, about 5–7 minutes, and season with the remainder of the spice mix. Combine the garbanzo beans and almonds in a serving bowl and garnish with the fried rosemary. **Serves 6–8.**

Grilled Prosciutto-Wrapped Asparagus

1 lb asparagus, ends trimmed
2 garlic cloves, minced
1 tbsp Parmigiano-Reggiano cheese, freshly grated
1 tbsp extra-virgin olive oil
1 tbsp lemon juice, freshly squeezed
Black pepper, freshly ground to taste
10 slices prosciutto, halved lengthwise

In a large Ziploc® bag, add all the ingredients except the prosciutto. Marinate the asparagus for a minimum of 1 hour or overnight. When ready to grill, wrap each spear with a piece of prosciutto and place on a hot, oiled grill. Cook until the prosciutto gets crispy and the asparagus is tender. Serve right away or at room temperature. **Serves 10.**

Market Salad with Herbed Vinaigrette

Discover the magic of the mandoline by slicing your vegetables into beautiful, thin ribbons for this salad.

1 shallot, minced
1 tbsp Dijon mustard
1 tbsp honey
1 tbsp lemon juice, freshly squeezed
2 tbsp white wine vinegar
Salt to taste
Black pepper, freshly ground to taste
⅓ cup extra-virgin olive oil
2 tbsp mixed fresh herbs such as dill, parsley, thyme, chives and tarragon, chopped
Seasonal greens and vegetables from the farmers market

In a small bowl, whisk together the shallot, mustard, honey, lemon juice, vinegar, salt and pepper. Slowly drizzle in the extra-virgin olive oil until emulsified. Stir in the herbs, taste and season again if necessary. Dress a mixture of greens and vegetables from your local farmers market and serve immediately. This dressing lasts up to a week in the refrigerator in a sealed container. **Serves 10.**

Basic Pizza Dough

1 packet active dry yeast
Pinch granulated sugar
1 ½ cups warm water, divided
3 ½ cups all-purpose flour
      plus extra for dusting

1 tbsp sea salt
1 tbsp extra-virgin olive oil, plus extra for greasing
Semolina flour, for dusting

In the bowl of a stand mixer, mix the active dry yeast, sugar and ½ cup of warm water (approximately 110–130 degrees). Let stand for 10 minutes to activate the yeast. You will notice that the mixture will become frothy and double in size. IMPORTANT: If this does not happen, either you've got a bad batch of yeast, or the water is too hot or cold. Without the yeast activated, the dough will not rise and your pizza will not pass muster.

Once the yeast is activated, add the rest of the water, flour, sugar, salt and extra-virgin olive oil. Using a stand mixer fitted with a dough hook attachment, mix on low speed 3–4 minutes, scraping down the sides and bottom of the bowl. Turn the speed up to medium-high and mix for another 3–4 minutes. Depending on the humidity in the air, you may need to add a bit more flour if the dough is too sticky. It should not be wet, but it should pull away from the sides of the bowl and form somewhat of a clump.

Next, oil the inside of a large bowl with extra-virgin olive oil. Scrape the pizza dough from the bowl of the stand mixer and place it on a floured cutting board. Knead it a few times to bring it together into a cohesive mass before placing it in the oiled bowl. Cover with plastic wrap and let rise in a warm place (80 degrees is ideal; I put mine next to the stove) for a minimum of 2 hours.

After the dough has risen, transfer it onto a floured cutting board. Using a knife, divide the ball into 4 equal pieces. Oil a sheet pan and place each new ball onto the pan and cover with plastic wrap. Let it rise again for another 2 hours. At this time, you can also put each dough ball into a small Ziploc bag and refrigerate or freeze for later.

Once the dough has risen, it is ready for pizza. Put the dough onto a floured cutting board and pat it into a disc. Using a rolling pin, roll the dough into a 12–14 inch round, making sure it is not sticking to the cutting board. You can also stretch the dough by hand, lifting and rotating it around your knuckles, while gravity does the work. Dust a pizza peel with some semolina flour and place the dough on top.

Top the pizza sparingly with the ingredients of your choice—see recipes for ideas. This dough is meant to be stretched thin and cook quickly, so less is more when it comes toppings. Cook in a wood-fired oven, grill or the hottest setting in your home oven equipped with a pizza stone (which should heat for 1 hour) until crispy. Eat pronto, and enjoy! **Makes 4 pizzas (12–14 inches each).**

For more about the amazing Louise, visit www.worldofweezy.com.

Classic Red Sauce

2 (28-oz) cans whole San Marzano tomatoes
10 fresh basil leaves
5 cloves garlic

Pinch crushed red pepper flakes
Pinch sugar
Salt to taste

Add all the ingredients to a pot and simmer over medium heat for 30 minutes. Pour into a blender or food processor and blend to a chunky sauce consistency. The sauce will last up to a week in the refrigerator and freezes well for later use. **Makes approximately 8 cups.**

Classic Pesto Sauce

1 medium-large bunch of basil, about 50 leaves
¼ cup Parmigiano-Reggiano cheese, freshly grated
¼ cup pine nuts, toasted
2–3 cloves garlic

Pinch crushed red pepper flakes
¼ cup extra-virgin olive oil
Squeeze of lemon
Salt, to taste

To the bowl of a food processor, add the basil, cheese, pine nuts, garlic and crushed red pepper flakes.
Pulse until well combined. While the machine is on, add the extra-virgin olive oil until a bright green chunky paste has formed. Add the lemon juice and pulse again. Add salt to taste.
Makes approximately 2 cups.

Margherita Pizza

1 pizza dough
3 tbsp Classic Red Sauce
2 oz fresh mozzarella cheese
Handful Pecorino Romano cheese, freshly grated
Handful Parmigiano-Reggiano cheese, freshly grated
Salt, to taste
Extra-virgin olive oil, for drizzle
Fresh basil, for garnish

Follow the directions in the pizza dough recipe. When you are ready to dress your pizza, start by spreading the red sauce over the crust. Add the fresh mozzarella and grate a nice dusting of the Pecorino over the top. Season with just a touch of salt. Slide the pizza into the oven and bake until crispy and bubbly. Pull the pizza out of the oven and grate some Parmigiano-Reggiano cheese on top. Add a drizzle of extra-virgin olive oil and top with fresh basil. Slice and serve immediately. **Serves 8.**

Heirloom Tomato & Pesto Pizza

1 pizza dough
3 tbsp Classic Pesto Sauce
2 oz fresh mozzarella cheese
4–5 slices of heirloom tomato
Handful Parmigiano-Reggiano cheese, freshly grated
Arugula, for garnish
Lemon, for drizzle
Extra-virgin olive oil, for drizzle
Salt, to taste
Black pepper, freshly ground to taste

Follow the directions in the pizza dough recipe. When you're ready to dress your pizza, start by spreading the pesto over the crust. Add the fresh mozzarella and follow with the tomato slices. Season with just a touch of salt. Slide the pizza into the oven and bake until crispy and bubbly. While the pizza is cooking, mix the arugula, a squirt of fresh lemon juice, a drizzle of extra-virgin olive oil and some fresh grated Parmigiano-Reggiano cheese in a bowl. Season to taste with salt and pepper. Pull the pizza out of the oven and cut into pieces. Top the pie with the arugula salad and eat immediately. **Serves 8.**

Sausage, Crispy Fennel & Sage Pizza

1 pizza dough
Extra-virgin olive oil, for sautéing
2 (3 oz) hot Italian sausages,
    casings removed
¼ bulb fennel, thinly sliced

4–5 sage leaves
3 tbsp Classic Red Sauce
2 oz fresh mozzarella cheese
Handful Pecorino Romano cheese, freshly grated
Handful Parmigiano-Reggiano cheese, freshly grated

In a sauté pan over medium-high heat, add a few tablespoons of extra-virgin olive oil and the sausage. Break up the sausage with a spoon and cook the sausage halfway through, remove from the pan and set aside. Immediately add the fennel to the sausage drippings and turn the heat down to medium. Cook until caramelized, about 15 minutes. Deglaze the bottom of the pan with a bit of water and scrape up all the browned bits from the bottom. Remove the fennel from the pan and set aside. Wipe the pan dry and add a shallow layer of extra-virgin olive oil to the pan. Once it is glistening, add the sage leaves and fry until crispy. Remove with a slotted spoon and drain on paper towels.

Follow the directions for pizza dough (see page 108). When you are ready to dress your pizza, start by spreading the red sauce over the crust. Add the fresh mozzarella, then the sausage and fennel. Grate some Pecorino Romano over the top, and slide the pizza into the oven. Bake until crispy and bubbly. Remove the pie from the oven and top with some grated Parmigiano-Reggiano cheese and the crispy sage leaves. Slice and serve immediately. **Serves 8.**

Broccolini, Mushroom & Fontina Pizza

1 pizza dough
1 oz fresh mozzarella cheese
1 oz Fontina cheese
Handful fresh broccolini, blanched
Handful fresh mushrooms, sliced
Handful Parmigiano-Reggiano cheese, freshly grated
Pinch crushed red pepper flakes
Extra-virgin olive oil, to drizzle
Salt, to taste

Follow the directions for pizza dough (see page 108). When you are ready to dress your pizza, start by adding the fresh mozzarella and Fontina. Follow with the broccolini and mushrooms. Season with salt and drizzle with extra-virgin olive oil. Bake until crispy and bubbly. Remove the pie from the oven and top with some grated Parmigiano-Reggiano cheese and crushed red pepper flakes. Slice and serve immediately. **Serves 8.**

Brie, Truffle Oil, Honey & Sea Salt Pizza

1 pizza dough
2 oz triple-crème Brie cheese
Extra-virgin olive oil, to drizzle
Truffle oil, to drizzle
Honey, to drizzle
Sea salt, to taste

Follow the directions for pizza dough (see page 108). When you are ready to dress your pizza, start by drizzling the dough with some extra-virgin olive oil. Bake in the oven until the dough sets. Pull it out, add the Brie and put back in the oven until cheese has just melted. Remove from the oven and drizzle with truffle oil and honey. Sprinkle with sea salt, slice and serve immediately. **Serves 8.**

Hot Soppressata, Pepper, Onion & Pepperoncini Pizza

1 pizza dough
3 tbsp Classic Red Sauce
2 oz fresh mozzarella cheese
1 oz soppressata salami, thinly sliced
1 fresh red, yellow or green bell pepper, thinly sliced
Handful red onion, thinly sliced
Handful Pecorino Romano cheese, freshly grated
Handful Parmigiano-Reggiano cheese, freshly grated
Handful pepperoncini, chopped

Follow the directions for pizza dough (see page 108). When you are ready to dress your pizza, start by spreading the red sauce over the crust. Add the fresh mozzarella, then the soppressata, peppers and onions. Grate some Pecorino over the top and slide the pizza into the oven. Bake until crispy and bubbly. Remove the pie from the oven and top with grated Parmigiano-Reggiano cheese and pepperoncini. Slice and serve immediately. **Serves 8.**

Blueberry Crisp with Almond Streusel

There's nothing more simple and satisfying than fresh fruit baked with a crumble topping. I use this wonderfully crunchy streusel not only on this blueberry crisp, but also as a topping on any baked fruit dessert.

FOR THE ALMOND STREUSEL:
¾ **cup granulated sugar, unleveled**
2 **cups all-purpose flour, scant**
¾ **cup finely ground almond meal flour, heaping**
12 **tbsp unsalted butter**

FOR THE FILLING:
4 **cups fresh blueberries, washed and dried**
½ **cup granulated sugar**
1 **tbsp lemon juice, freshly squeezed**
1 **tsp lemon zest**

Preheat oven to 375 degrees.

FOR THE STREUSEL: In a medium bowl, combine sugar, all-purpose flour and almond flour and mix thoroughly. Cut in butter until mixture becomes a coarse crumb. Set aside.

FOR THE FILLING: In a medium bowl, use a spatula to gently toss together the blueberries, sugar, lemon juice and lemon zest. Let mixture sit for about 15 minutes. Place blueberry mixture into a 1 ½-quart baking dish and cover completely with Almond Streusel. Bake for approximately 45 minutes, until top is browned and berry filling is bubbling. Serve with homemade Vanilla Bean Ice Cream (see recipe on page 121).

NOTE: This streusel makes enough for 2 (9-inch) pies or 2 blueberry crisps. If you only plan to make one, freeze the remainder for later use on your morning yogurt or evening ice cream. **Serves 8.**

Strawberry Ice Cream

Here's a secret you'll be glad I shared: use only really ripe, sweet strawberries like Harry's (legendary!) Berries to infuse this ice cream with a deep, complex berry taste. Their strawberries are the sweetest, most fragrant berries we've ever tasted—and totally worth the trouble of getting to the Beverly Hills Farmers Market *before* it opens on Sunday morning.

If you're lucky enough to grab some before they sell out, they're delicious right out of the carton... and life-changing in homemade ice cream. If you don't have access to Harry's, buy some small organic strawberries from your local farmers market.

1 cup heavy cream
½ cup half & half
¾ cup granulated sugar, divided
3 large egg yolks, room temperature
2 ¾ cups fresh organic strawberries, washed, dried and hulled

In heavy saucepan over medium heat, combine the heavy cream and the half & half until scalded. In a small bowl, add ½ cup of granulated sugar and the egg yolks and whisk until lemon-colored. Pour egg mixture into cream and cook over low heat, stirring constantly until mixture begins to thicken enough to coat the back of a spoon. Do not let custard boil, as it will curdle. Remove saucepan from heat and place it in a roasting pan filled with ice and water to accelerate cooling. Stir in saucepan until custard is completely cool. Transfer custard to an 8-cup Pyrex measuring beaker with handle and spout. Cover and chill for several hours.

About 30 minutes prior to freezing, purée the strawberries in a blender until very smooth. Use remaining ¼ cup of sugar to sprinkle over the strawberry purée and let sit for 30 minutes until sugar dissolves. Add custard to the purée and stir until just combined. Pour into ice cream maker and freeze according to manufacturer's instructions. **Makes 1 large quart.**

Vanilla Bean Ice Cream

2 whole soft vanilla beans
2 ½ cups half & half
⅔ cup granulated sugar

4 large egg yolks, lightly beaten
1 cup heavy cream

Split vanilla beans in half lengthwise, scrape seeds, and add pods and seeds to a heavy saucepan. Add half & half. Cook over medium heat until very warm but not boiling. In a small bowl, whisk together the sugar and egg yolks, then add ½ cup of the hot half & half into the mixture to thin. Pour thinned mixture back into saucepan and continue stirring until well blended. Cook custard over medium low heat until mixture begins to thicken enough to coat the back of a spoon. Do not let custard boil, as it will curdle. Remove saucepan from heat and place it in a roasting pan filled with ice and water to accelerate cooling. Stir custard in saucepan to cool completely, then stir in the remaining cup of heavy cream. Pour thickened custard through a fine mesh sieve into an 8-cup Pyrex measuring beaker with a handle and spout. Place vanilla bean pods back in the custard, cover and chill for several hours. Remember to remove vanilla bean pods prior to freezing in an ice cream maker. Pour into ice cream maker and freeze according to manufacturer's instructions. **Makes 1 quart.**

Luscious Lemon Ice Cream

Trust me: few desserts are as perfectly summery as homemade lemon ice cream. The combination of zest and juice from a variety of lemons growing in our yard gives this recipe an intense and totally unique citrus flavor.

1 ¼ cups granulated sugar
6 large egg yolks
2 tbsp lemon zest (I use 1 Meyer lemon and 1 regular lemon)
¾ cup lemon juice, freshly squeezed (I use equal parts Meyer lemon and regular lemon)

2 cups heavy cream, divided
2 cups half & half

In medium bowl, whisk together the sugar, egg yolks and lemon zest. Set aside. In heavy saucepan, heat 1 cup of the cream with the half & half over medium-high heat until it begins to lightly simmer. Reduce heat to low. Pour some of the cream mixture into yolks to thin, whisk and then return thinned yolk mixture to saucepan and continue to stir until mixture begins to thicken enough to coat the back of a spoon, approximately 10 minutes. Do not to let custard boil, as it will curdle. Remove saucepan from heat and place it in a roasting pan filled with ice and water to accelerate cooling. Pour thickened custard through a fine mesh sieve into an 8-cup Pyrex measuring beaker with handle and spout—this will make it much easier to pour into the ice cream maker. Stir in remaining cup of cream and lemon juice, and cover and chill for several hours. Pour into ice cream maker and freeze according to manufacturer's instructions. **Makes 2 quarts.**

Ferne Dickey's Ginger Snaps

Years ago, my friend Andi shared this recipe from her grandmother's friend Ferne Dickey. Even the most serious ginger snap enthusiasts insist that these soft, chewy and spicy cookies are their favorite. Around our house, these cookies are referred to simply as Ferne Dickeys.

¾ cup unsalted margarine, melted

1 cup granulated sugar, plus extra for sprinkling

¼ cup molasses

1 egg

2 cups all-purpose flour

2 tsp baking soda

½ tsp ground cloves

3 tsp ground ginger

1 tsp ground cinnamon

½ tsp salt

Use an electric mixer to beat together margarine, sugar, molasses and egg. In a separate bowl, whisk together all of the dry ingredients. Add to molasses mixture and mix until a smooth dough forms. Cover and chill for several hours until dough is cold enough to handle. Preheat oven to 325 degrees. Line baking sheets with parchment paper. Use a small ice cream scoop or your hands to make 1-inch balls. Place on prepared baking sheets 2 inches apart. Bake for 8–10 minutes. While cookies are hot, sprinkle with granulated sugar.

NOTE: Using margarine gives these cookies their chewy texture—substituting butter will not yield the same consistency/results. **Makes 24 cookies.**

Butter Crisp Sugar Cookies

1 cup unsalted butter

1 cup confectioner's sugar, plus extra for dusting

1 large egg

1 ½ tsp pure vanilla extract

2 ½ cups all-purpose flour

½ tsp salt

Preheat oven to 350 degrees. Lightly grease 2 baking sheets. Using an electric mixer, cream butter until soft and fluffy. Add sugar and continue to mix. Blend in egg and vanilla. In a small bowl sift together flour and salt and blend into creamed mixture until thoroughly mixed. Chill dough for at least 30 minutes. On a lightly-floured board, roll out dough to desired thickness and cut into shapes with cookie cutters. Place on prepared baking sheet and bake for 10–12 minutes until lightly browned. Let cool completely on wire racks and lightly dust with confectioner's sugar. **Makes approximately 30 cookies.**

Small Bites & Big Drinks

I believe that cocktail hour—the languorous act of unwinding oneself from the tight spool of the day, over casual nibbles and drinks—has become a lost art. And, as a passionate patron of this particular art, I've distilled my entertaining manifesto down to three words: *size does matter.*

At Honeysuckle Hill, we like our drinks big and our bites small. After all, a generous pour makes for a happy guest, and bite-sized hors d'oeuvres will never separate one from one's drink. By all accounts, Honeysuckle Hill's most famous past resident, Bette Davis, would have agreed. Bette's parties were legendary, and we hope our guests (and yours) will feel a bit of her feisty spirit when they sip the cocktail she inspired.

Cocktails
Honeysuckle Hill Cocktail

The Bumpy Night Cocktail

Nibbles
Sunset Ranch Marinated Olives

Sweet & Spicy Pistachios

Savory Cheese Crisps

Whole Baked Salami with Apricot Dipping Sauce

Bites
Chicken Satay with Spicy Peanut Dipping Sauce

Parmesan Puffs with Shrimp or Sun-Dried Tomato

Crispy Sage Leaves

Oven-Baked Sweet Potato Fries

Mini Sirloin Sliders with Poncho's Sauce

Rich, Creamy Macaroni & Cheese

Sweets
Lime Sugar Cookies

Cinnamon Apple Swirl Bundt Cake

Bread Pudding with Bourbon Pecan Sauce

Chocolate Crème Brûlée

Honeysuckle Hill Cocktail

½ cup honey

1 cup lemon juice, freshly squeezed

2 cups honeysuckle-infused vodka (recipe follows)
　　　or white rum

1 bunch fresh basil

1 liter seltzer water

1 fresh lemon, sliced into rounds

In a large pitcher, combine the honey, lemon juice, alcohol and a handful of basil. Stir well and refrigerate for a minimum of 2 hours. After the flavors have married, add the seltzer, lemon slices and ice. Serve immediately. **Serves 8.**

FOR THE HONEYSUCKLE-INFUSED VODKA:

2 (750-ml) bottles 100-proof vodka

4–5 cups of fresh honeysuckle blossoms (no leaves or stems)

Use a ½ gallon glass mason jar with a lid. Pour vodka into jar, add honeysuckle blossoms and seal jar. Store in a cool place and allow blossoms to soak in vodka for 3 days. The flowers will begin to brown and the liquid will turn a light amber color. Strain vodka through a fine cheesecloth and discard blossoms. Vodka should be clean of debris. Pour vodka into bottles or jars. Store in the refrigerator until ready to use—it will keep its flavor for up to 3 weeks. **Makes approximately ½ gallon.**

The Bumpy Night Cocktail

Inspired by Ms. Davis and her signature line from "All About Eve." We like to serve this cocktail with one enormous, crystal-clear ice ball—a small detail that makes a big impression, as it keeps drinks undiluted and Arctic-cold.

½ tsp blood orange bitters (approximately 4 dashes)

1 tsp granulated sugar

1 slice fresh blood orange (or regular orange)

1 splash seltzer water

2 oz bourbon

Fresh orange slices and orange blossoms,
　　　for garnish

In the bottom of a shaker, muddle together the bitters, sugar, orange slice and seltzer. Add the bourbon and ice and shake well. Strain over a large ice ball or ice cube and garnish with an orange slice and/or fresh orange blossom. **Makes 1 individual serving.**

Sunset Ranch Marinated Olives

Our dear friends Dan and Nanette are literally living the California dream, on a ranch high in the mountains above Malibu. They are known for their amazing farm dinners, to which friends and neighbors always show up with wonderful contributions from their own gardens and kitchens. We were fortunate to get a taste of these olives at a recent Sunset Ranch gathering.

1 cup extra-virgin olive oil

4 garlic cloves, peeled

Peel of 1 lemon

4 slices of fresh orange, thin wedges

2 fresh rosemary sprigs

1 tsp smoked paprika

½ tsp crushed red pepper flakes

1 quart mixed Greek olives

1 cup feta cheese, well drained and cut into ½-inch cubes (optional)

In a saucepan over low heat, combine the oil, garlic, lemon peel, orange slices, rosemary sprigs, paprika and chili flakes. Warm until heated through and flavors are blended. Toss warm liquid with olives and stir to coat evenly. If using feta cheese, add after mixture is completely cooled. Serve at room temperature. Will keep in refrigerator for up to a week. **Serves 10.**

Sweet & Spicy Pistachios

These are truly addictive and they are a great nibble to serve with cocktails. Plan on making an extra batch as you'll eat the first ones long before your company arrives.

2 cups raw shelled pistachios

½ cup confectioner's sugar

24 oz vegetable oil, for frying

Sea salt, to taste

Cayenne pepper, to taste

Fill a medium sauce pot halfway with water and bring to a heavy boil. Drop the nuts in boiling water for 2 minutes to blanch. Drain and immediately toss with confectioner's sugar, mixing well to evenly coat.

Pour enough oil into a heavy skillet to reach a depth of 1 ½ inches and heat to 375 degrees. NOTE: You will not need to use all of the oil. Using a slotted spoon, add sugared nuts in small batches, and fry until crisp and golden brown—approximately 1-2 minutes. Remove nuts from oil with a slotted spoon and transfer to a fine-mesh splatter screen to drain—DO NOT use paper towels, as they will stick. Allow the oil to come back to temperature between batches. While nuts are still warm, sprinkle with salt and cayenne pepper to taste. When completely cool, store in an airtight container for up to a week. **Serves 6–8.**

Savory Cheese Crisps

8 tbsp unsalted butter, room temperature

6 oz Parmigiano-Reggiano cheese, freshly grated

1 ½ tsp fresh minced herbs (I use thyme, but any combination will work)

½ tsp salt

½ tsp black pepper, freshly ground

1 tbsp heavy cream

1 cup all-purpose flour

Use an electric mixer to cream the butter for about 1 minute. Add the cheese, herbs, salt and pepper, and blend until just combined.

Add the cream and flour, and mix until just combined. Place dough on a sheet of plastic wrap, gently form into a ball and cover completely with plastic. Refrigerate dough for 30 minutes.

Preheat the oven to 350 degrees. Lightly flour a baking sheet. When dough is thoroughly chilled, place in the center of a lightly floured board. Roll dough evenly until it's approximately ¼ inch thick. Using a small shaped cookie cutter, cut out small crackers and place on prepared baking sheet. You will need to re-roll the dough at least one or two more times to use all of it. Bake for approximately 15 minutes until crisps begin to slightly brown on edges only. Cool on wire rack before serving. **Makes approximately 36 small crackers.**

Whole Baked Salami with Apricot Dipping Sauce

I love to serve this old-school Midwestern staple alongside its nouvelle California cousins—it's sweet, savory, crispy and kosher to boot.

1 whole soft kosher salami

1 cup apricot preserves

⅓ cup Dijon mustard

⅓ cup apricot liqueur

Preheat oven to 350 degrees. Cross score salami about one ¼ way through from the top and place with scored side up on a slotted broiling pan. In a small saucepan, combine preserves, mustard and liqueur and cook over medium heat until warm. Pour half of the sauce over the salami, reserving the remaining half for dipping sauce. Bake salami until well heated through, about 10 minutes. Serve salami whole with knives for cutting and toothpicks for dipping into sauce. **Serves 8–10.**

Another unique find: our Victorian porcupine toothpick holder. In those days, toothpicks were made from real porcupine quills—and were used for actually picking teeth, right there at the dinner table! Today, thank goodness, they're used mainly for testing cakes and spearing hors d'oeuvres.

Chicken Satay

4 tbsp soy sauce
1 tbsp fresh ginger, finely chopped
1 small shallot, chopped
2 garlic cloves, pressed
1 tbsp dark brown sugar, firmly packed
1 tbsp lime juice, freshly squeezed
1 tsp ground coriander
1 tsp chili paste
24 pieces chicken breast, skinless, boneless and cut into 1-inch cubes
1 bunch green onions, tops removed, cut on the diagonal into 1-inch spears
12 skewers
Spicy Peanut Dipping Sauce (recipe follows)

In a medium bowl, combine the first 8 ingredients and mix well. Add chicken and toss well to coat each piece. Cover and refrigerate for 1 hour. To assemble kabobs, place one piece of chicken on the skewer, follow with a spear of green onion and top with another piece of chicken. Place skewers over very hot grill, turning once until browned on both sides—about 5 minutes. Serve with Spicy Peanut Dipping Sauce. **Serves 6.**

Spicy Peanut Dipping Sauce

¼ cup creamy peanut butter
2 tbsp rice vinegar
2 tbsp soy sauce
1 clove garlic, pressed
1 tsp sesame oil
1 tsp chili oil
⅛ tsp crushed red pepper flakes
1 small green onion, thinly sliced

In a small pot, combine all ingredients together. Mix well and heat for 8 minutes over medium low flame until warm. Serve immediately. **Makes approximately ⅔ cup.**

Parmesan Puffs with Shrimp or Sun-Dried Tomato

8 slices white bread
½ cup Parmigiano-Reggiano cheese, finely grated
½ cup mayonnaise
1 tbsp fresh chives, finely minced
Black pepper, freshly ground to taste
32 cooked baby shrimp or ¾ cup sun-dried tomato strips

Preheat oven to 350 degrees. Using a 1 ½-inch diameter round cookie cutter, cut circles of bread out of each slice and discard crusts. Each slice will yield 4 rounds. Place bread rounds in a single layer on ungreased baking sheet. Toast slightly in oven until they begin to brown. Remove from oven and let cool on a baking sheet.

Adjust oven rack to top shelf position and set oven to broil. In a small bowl, combine cheese, mayonnaise, chives and black pepper and blend well. Spread a thin layer of cheese mixture on top of each toasted bread round. Place either a baby shrimp or a slice of sun-dried tomato on top. Cover with a small dollop of cheese mixture. Place baking sheet under broiler just until cheese begins to bubble and brown. Serve immediately. **Makes 32 puffs.**

Crispy Sage Leaves

1 large bunch fresh sage leaves
1 ½ cups all-purpose flour
1 can domestic beer
1 cup vegetable oil, for frying
Sea salt, to taste

Rinse sage leaves and dry thoroughly with paper towel. Place flour in a medium bowl and pour only a small amount of the beer into the flour, using a whisk to mix. Continue adding the beer slowly, a little at a time, just until the batter becomes thick enough to coat the leaves. You will not need much.

Heat oil in small stock pot until very hot (approximately 350 degrees). Dip leaves in batter to coat, let excess batter drip off and drop leaves into hot oil. Watch closely: if the temperature is correct, they should be done in one minute. Remove from oil with a slotted spoon and drain on paper towels. Sprinkle with a pinch of sea salt and serve warm. **Serves 6.**

Oven-Baked Sweet Potato Fries

4 medium sweet potatoes (orange-flesh yams), skin left on, cut into ½ inch sticks
¼ cup extra-virgin olive oil
1 tsp sea salt, plus extra for sprinkling on top
½ tsp black pepper, freshly ground
½ tsp ground cumin

Preheat oven to 425 degrees. In a large bowl, combine oil, salt, pepper and cumin. Add potatoes and toss well to coat evenly. Place potatoes in a single layer on two large ungreased rimmed baking sheets. Bake for 15–20 minutes, and then use a spatula to flip potatoes over. Continue baking for another 15–20 minutes until potatoes are crispy and brown on both sides. Sprinkle with salt and serve immediately. **Serves 8.**

Mini Sirloin Sliders

1 lb fresh ground sirloin, room temperature
Lawry's Seasoned Salt, to taste
Black pepper, freshly ground to taste
Garlic powder, to taste
Onion powder, to taste

5 (4-inch) slices cheddar cheese, quartered
18–20 mini brioche or mini hamburger buns
1 small bunch fresh arugula, for garnish
Poncho's Sauce (recipe follows)

Gently shape meat into 18–20 equal-sized balls. Press down lightly to make small but thick patties. Place patties in a shallow baking dish and season with salt, pepper, garlic powder and onion powder. Cook on a hot grill for approximately 8 minutes per side, until burgers have a nice crust but are still pink in the center. Place cheese slices over each burger and cook for an additional 2 minutes until cheese just begins to melt. Remove from grill and place on buns. Top with a dollop of Poncho's sauce and a few sprigs of arugula for garnish. **Makes 18–20 mini sliders.**

Poncho's Sauce

This is our interpretation of Chef Poncho's zesty signature sauce from Detroit's legendary London Chop House. It's a great complement to our Mini Sliders or any seafood.

½ cup ketchup
½ cup chili sauce
3 tbsp mayonnaise
2 tbsp fresh horseradish, grated
2 ½ tbsp honey
1 tbsp capers, drained and minced
1 tbsp whole-grain mustard
1 tbsp pineapple juice
1 tbsp lemon juice, freshly squeezed
1 tbsp white vinegar

1 tbsp dry mustard
½ tbsp ground ginger
1 tsp fennel seeds, finely ground
½ tbsp fresh garlic, minced
½ tbsp Worcestershire sauce
2 tsp yellow onion, grated
½ tsp Tabasco sauce
¼ tsp salt
Black pepper, coarsely ground, to taste

In a medium bowl, combine all ingredients together and mix thoroughly. Adjust Tabasco, salt and pepper as needed. Cover and refrigerate for at least two days prior to use. Will keep for up to a month in the refrigerator. **Makes approximately 2 cups.**

Rich, Creamy Macaroni & Cheese

8 oz elbow macaroni noodles or fusilli noodles
2 tbsp unsalted butter
2 tbsp all-purpose flour
1 tsp salt
½ tsp ground white pepper
1 ½ tsp dried minced onion flakes
½ tsp garlic powder
1 cup whole milk
1 cup half & half
½ cup heavy cream
4 oz sharp cheddar cheese, grated
4 oz Velveeta cheese, cut in small cubes
1 cup Parmigiano-Reggiano cheese, freshly grated, plus extra for sprinkling

Preheat oven to 350 degrees. In a large pot, cook noodles in boiling water until al dente. Drain well and set aside.

In a medium saucepan, melt butter over low heat. Add flour, salt, pepper, dried onion flakes and garlic powder and stir until just combined. Add milk, half & half and cream and whisk until smooth. Increase heat slightly and whisk constantly until mixture begins to thicken. Add cheeses and whisk until melted and smooth.

Remove from heat. Stir in cooked pasta noodles, being sure to coat evenly. Transfer noodles to a baking dish (8-inch or 9-inch square works well, or use individual ramekins). Sprinkle additional grated Parmigiano-Reggiano cheese evenly over top.

Bake for 30 minutes or until lightly browned and bubbly. **Serves 6–8.**

Lime Sugar Cookies

¾ cup unsalted butter, softened

2 cups granulated sugar, divided

Zest of 1 ½ limes, divided

½ cup sour cream

2 large egg yolks, room temperature

2 tsp lime juice, freshly squeezed

½ tsp salt

2 tsp baking powder

2 ½ cups all-purpose flour

Preheat oven to 300 degrees. Line 2 baking sheets with parchment paper. Use an electric mixer to beat together butter, 1 ½ cups sugar and zest of 1 lime until lightly creamed. Add sour cream and egg yolks and beat until just blended.

Add lime juice and continue to mix, scraping down sides of bowl. Add salt, baking powder and flour and beat until blended. Cover and chill dough for one hour.

In a small bowl, combine remaining sugar and lime zest and set aside. Use a small ice cream scoop to scoop out balls of dough and place on prepared baking sheet 2 inches apart.

Bake for 18 minutes or less, only until edges begin to lightly brown. Remove from oven. While cookies are still hot, lightly sprinkle with sugar/lime zest mixture. Cool before serving.
Makes 24 cookies.

Cinnamon Apple Swirl Bundt Cake

FOR THE CINNAMON/APPLE FILLING:

3 large apples (I use Honeycrisp, Fuji or Granny Smith)

2 tbsp granulated sugar

1 ½ tsp ground cinnamon

¾ cup Baker's cinnamon filling mix (available online from King Arthur Flour Co.)

3 tbsp water

FOR THE CAKE:

2 cups granulated sugar

1 cup vegetable oil

4 large eggs, room temperature

¼ cup orange juice, freshly squeezed

2 tsp pure vanilla extract

3 cups all-purpose flour

1 tbsp baking powder

¼ tsp salt

Preheat oven to 325 degrees. Grease a 12-cup bundt pan (or use two 6-cup bundt pans to make 2 smaller cakes).

FOR THE FILLING: Peel, core and chop apples into small chunks (approximately ½ to ¾ inch). Place apples in a medium bowl and toss with cinnamon and sugar. Set aside. In a separate small bowl, mix the Baker's cinnamon filling mix with water until it becomes a smooth paste. Set aside.

FOR THE CAKE: Use an electric mixer to beat together sugar, vegetable oil, eggs, orange juice and vanilla. In a separate small bowl, sift together flour, baking powder and salt. Slowly add dry ingredients to batter, beating until smooth.

Spoon ⅓ of the cake batter into prepared pan and top with a few spoonfuls of cinnamon paste. Gently run a knife through the batter to slightly swirl the paste. Sprinkle with ½ of the apple mixture. Add next ⅓ of batter, top with remaining cinnamon paste and again swirl through the cake batter with a knife. Sprinkle with remaining apple mixture and cover with remaining ⅓ of cake batter. Bake for 1 hour or until cake tester comes out clean. Cool for at least 30 minutes before removing from pan.

NOTE: This cake is best when made the day BEFORE you plan to serve it. When cake is completely cooled, store in an airtight container. **Serves 16.**

Bread Pudding with Bourbon Pecan Sauce

FOR THE PUDDING:
1 lb loaf of raisin challah or brioche bread, cut into small cubes
2 ½ tbsp ground cinnamon
6 tbsp unsalted butter, melted
3 cups half & half
6 large eggs
1 ½ cups granulated sugar
2 tsp pure vanilla extract
Pinch salt

FOR THE BOURBON PECAN SAUCE:
8 tbsp unsalted butter
1 cup heavy cream
1 tsp pure vanilla extract
1 ½ cups dark brown sugar, firmly packed
1 lb pecans, lightly toasted
¼ cup bourbon

FOR THE PUDDING: Preheat oven to 350 degrees. Line a baking sheet with aluminum foil. In a large bowl, combine bread cubes and cinnamon. Drizzle with butter and toss until evenly coated. Spread bread cubes into a single layer on prepared baking sheet and bake for 15 minutes until lightly toasted.

Pour half & half into a large saucepan and cook over medium heat. Lower heat and simmer for another 5 minutes. In a large bowl, whisk together eggs, sugar, vanilla and salt. Add the warm half & half slowly to the egg mixture, a little at a time, and whisk until smooth. Add bread cubes and stir until liquid is absorbed. Cover and refrigerate in the bowl for 8 hours.

Grease 8 (4 ¼-inch wide by 2-inch deep) ramekins. Divide bread pudding evenly into prepared ramekins. Place ramekins in a roasting pan and fill the pan halfway with water. Bake for 40 minutes. Serve warm with bourbon pecan sauce.

FOR THE SAUCE: Melt butter in a small saucepan over medium heat. Add cream, vanilla and sugar and bring to a boil, whisking constantly. Reduce heat and simmer for 5 minutes. Stir in pecans and bourbon and continue to simmer for another 5 minutes. Serve warm, drizzled over bread pudding.

Can also be made in a 9x13 baking dish. **Makes 8 individual bread puddings.**

Chocolate Crème Brûlée

6 cups heavy cream

2 whole soft vanilla beans

¾ lb bittersweet chocolate, chopped

¼ cup Dutch cocoa powder

¼ cup ground espresso or coffee powder

16 egg yolks

5 ¼ oz dark brown sugar, firmly packed

5 ¼ oz granulated sugar

1 cup whole milk

2 tsp pure vanilla extract

8 tbsp granulated sugar, for caramelizing tops

Preheat oven to 300 degrees. In heavy saucepan, combine cream and vanilla beans and bring to a boil—remove from heat. While warm, stir chocolate, cocoa powder and espresso powder into cream and blend until chocolate is melted and mixture is smooth. Set aside.

In a large bowl, whisk together egg yolks, sugars, milk and vanilla. Add to chocolate mixture while constantly whisking. Strain mixture through a fine-mesh sieve.

Pour into 12 ramekins or 36 mini ramekins. Fill a large roasting pan with a shallow layer of water (level should be approximately half the height of ramekins) and set desserts gently in pan. Cover with aluminum foil and bake for approximately 1 hour or until set. Let cool to room temperature uncovered. Chill in refrigerator until firm. To serve, sprinkle tops with granulated sugar and caramelize with propane torch or oven broiler. Serve immediately. **Serves 12–36 depending upon size of ramekin.**

Thanksgiving

I grew up in a place governed by seasons and traditions; we relied upon the changing leaves and crisp, chilly air to herald the arrival of autumn. Our holidays began in the kitchen, where we were never more than a few steps away from our collective past. Los Angeles, by contrast, lives in a hazy 72-degree daydream. It's a tireless engine of turnover and trend, yearning ever forward—and never looking back.

But perhaps more than anything else, Los Angeles is a place to reinvent oneself. And so, starting with Thanksgiving, we set about creating our own traditions. We built an adopted family out of friends and neighbors, and brought our feast out into the warm California breeze. Every year, I'm thankful that these handed-down holiday recipes help me bring a treasured part of my past to the table. Whether your meal is served indoors or al fresco, this day is about gratitude: for mementos of the past, connecting with loved ones in the present... and memories to cherish in the future.

Starters
Devils on Horseback

Chopped Kale Salad with Pomegranate Seeds,
      Pine Nuts & Parmesan

Holiday Favorites
Turkey Breast with Mustard & Black
      Peppercorn Crust

Herbed Mushroom Stuffing

New York Strip Roast

Popovers

Baked Apple Yams (Yapples)

Cran-Raspberry Jell-O Ring

Creamed Spinach

Green Beans with Caramelized Onions

Desserts
Chocolate Pecan Pie

Pumpkin Chiffon Pie

Apple Crumb Pie

Lemon Meringue Pie

Bourbon Pecan Pie with Spice Crust

Devils on Horseback

The appetizer **Angels on Horseback**—originally, smoked oysters wrapped in bacon—dates back to Victorian England. During its journey through time, the dish turned devilish, swapping the central oyster for a prune. Thankfully, in its trip across the Atlantic, it became the savory-sweet, oh-so-seventies staple we know today: bacon-wrapped dates stuffed with cheese.

18 dried Deglet Noor dates, pitted
1 (4-oz) block Parmigiano-Reggiano cheese, cut into small chunks
1 (16-oz) package uncooked sliced bacon

Using a sharp knife, cut a slit lengthwise in the center of each date. Cut cheese into almond-sized chunks. Place a piece of cheese inside each date and press edges of date around to cover it. Cut each strip of bacon in half. Wrap date with ½ slice of bacon and secure with a toothpick. Place on broiling pan with slots (so fat is able to drain) and broil in oven, turning over halfway through to brown both sides. Serve warm. **Makes 18 dates.**

Chopped Kale Salad with Pomegranate Seeds, Pine Nuts & Parmesan

4 oz Lacinato kale
½ cup fresh pomegranate seeds or dried currants
½ cup Parmigiano-Reggiano cheese, freshly grated
½ cup pine nuts, lightly toasted
4 tbsp extra-virgin olive oil
2 tbsp lemon juice, freshly squeezed
Salt, to taste

Wash and dry kale leaves. Cut away thick center rib of kale leaves and discard. Roll leaves tightly like a cigar and cut with a very sharp knife into fine strips. Place in a medium bowl. Add pomegranate seeds or currants, cheese and pine nuts to kale. In a separate small bowl, whisk together oil, lemon juice and a pinch of salt. Drizzle dressing over salad and toss well to coat.

NOTE: If you're using dried currants, soak them in hot water for 30 minutes and then drain well before adding to salad. **Serves 4–6.**

Turkey Breast with Mustard & Black Peppercorn Crust

1 (4-lb) whole turkey breast
½ cup Dijon mustard
¼ cup whole black peppercorns
3 cups fresh apple cider

Preheat oven to 350 degrees. Bring turkey breast to room temperature before starting. Wash turkey breast and pat dry with paper towel. Fill base of roasting pan with apple cider. On rack of roasting pan, place turkey breast-side up and completely coat with Dijon mustard.

Using a mortar and pestle, crush peppercorns until broken into small bits. Press crushed pepper into mustard, being sure to cover entire breast to form an even crust. Flip breast over so that breast side is down to begin baking. Place on middle rack and baste frequently with apple cider. Turkey will need to be turned over halfway through baking. Bake for 1 hour 20 minutes. **Serves 8.**

Herbed Mushroom Stuffing

6 tbsp salted butter
1 yellow onion, chopped
¾ lb fresh white button mushrooms, sliced
1 cup fresh celery, chopped
½ tsp salt
½ tsp black pepper, freshly ground

½ tsp poultry seasoning
¼ cup fresh parsley, finely chopped
1 loaf of fresh white bakery bread
1 (14-oz) bag Pepperidge Farm® original flavor herbed stuffing mix
1 cup chicken broth, as needed

Preheat oven to 325 degrees. Grease a 9x13 baking dish. In a large skillet, over medium heat, melt butter. Add onions and sauté until soft and glossy. Add mushrooms and celery. Season with salt, pepper and poultry seasoning. Sauté another 5 minutes until soft, but not too brown. Stir in parsley. Set aside.

Slice bread, remove crusts and cut into 1-inch cubes. In a large bowl, combine stuffing mix with bread cubes. Add sautéed vegetables to dry ingredients and gently toss with a spatula. Add chicken broth in small amounts just to moisten the mixture. Be careful not to add too much liquid, or the stuffing will become wet and heavy. Place in prepared baking dish and cover with foil. Bake for 30 minutes. **Serves 8.**

New York Strip Roast

1 (4-lb) whole boneless prime New York
    strip roast, fat trimmed
¼ cup unsalted butter, melted

¼ cup vegetable oil
2–3 tbsp black pepper, coarsely ground
2 tbsp kosher salt

Preheat oven to 350 degrees. In a small bowl, mix together butter and oil. In another small bowl combine pepper and salt. Coat both sides of strip roast with butter/oil mixture and then coat with pepper/salt mixture. Place meat on slotted broiling pan and roast for approximately 1 hour to achieve medium doneness. Test with a meat thermometer which should read 140 when inserted in the center.

NOTE: 15–20 minutes per pound will yield a roast that is cooked to medium doneness. **Serves 8.**

Popovers

6 tbsp unsalted butter, melted and divided
2 large eggs
1 cup whole milk

1 tsp granulated sugar
¼ tsp salt
1 cup all-purpose flour

Preheat oven to 400 degrees. Prepare a 6-cup popover pan by placing ⅓ teaspoon of melted butter into each of the popover wells. Using an electric mixer, beat eggs well. Add milk, 1 tablespoon of butter, sugar, salt and flour. Beat just until batter becomes smooth. Fill each cup ⅔ full with batter and bake for 20 minutes. Reduce oven temperature to 375 degrees and continue to bake for another 20 minutes until popovers are puffed and golden brown.

You can add freshly grated cheese, chopped chives or any combination of herbs and cheese to make these more flavorful and savory. **Serves 6.**

Baked Apple Yams (Yapples)

A fun twist on the casserole-dish staple, Yapples not only elevate the presentation of traditional sweet potatoes—they also have a tangy depth of flavor, thanks to the Granny Smith apples.

6–8 Granny Smith apples, medium size
2 (15-oz) cans unsweetened sweet potatoes
¼ cup dark brown sugar, firmly packed
½ cup unsalted butter, melted and divided
1 tsp salt

¼ cup orange juice, freshly squeezed
¼ tsp ground cinnamon
½ tsp orange zest
1 cup miniature marshmallows

Preheat oven to 350 degrees. Butter a 9x13 baking dish. Make apple shells by cutting and removing a circle in the tops of apples as you would begin to prepare a pumpkin for carving. Discard the tops. Use a melon baller to scoop out apples, leaving a ½-inch thick shell all around. Place apple shells in prepared baking dish.

In a medium bowl, mash the sweet potatoes with sugar, ¼ cup of the butter, salt, orange juice, cinnamon and orange zest. Stuff apple shells with sweet potato mixture until overflowing. Bake for 30 minutes until soft, basting with reserved ¼ cup of butter. Be careful not to overbake, or they will get soggy and lose their shape. When finished baking, sprinkle marshmallows over the apple tops. Place under broiler briefly, just until marshmallows are lightly browned. Serve warm.
Serves 6–8.

One more thing to be thankful for every year: finding this marvelous set of holiday china on eBay! These dishes survived more than a hundred years of gathering and good cheer before becoming part of our family—we hope we'll use them for a hundred more.

Cran-Raspberry Jell-O Ring

I like to believe I live in a world where one can serve Jell-O without irony. And so I happily whip up this smooth, fruity treat every year, as an alternative to traditional cranberry sauce. Here is what I have learned from the experience: even the naysayers are silent when their mouths are full. This dish is not only a Thanksgiving favorite, but is requested often throughout the year.

2 (3-oz) boxes instant raspberry-flavored Jell-O mix
1 cup boiling water
½ cup ice-cold water
1 (14-oz) can Ocean Spray® Jellied Cran-Raspberry Cranberry Sauce
1 cup sour cream
4 oz fresh raspberries, for garnish

Generously grease a 6-cup Jell-O ring mold with a paper towel dipped lightly in vegetable oil.

In a medium bowl, add gelatin mix to boiling water and stir until dissolved. Add the ice-cold water and set aside. Place the cran-raspberry sauce and sour cream in blender and purée until smooth. Add the gelatin mixture and continue to purée until smooth. Unless you have an extra-large blender, you may need to blend in two batches.

Pour Jell-O mixture into prepared ring. Cover with plastic wrap and chill until firm—at least 8 hours.

To unmold, run a knife along edge of ring for easier removal and invert onto serving platter. Fill center with fresh raspberries to garnish.

NOTE: If your local market doesn't carry the cran-raspberry sauce, plain jellied cranberry sauce will work just as well. **Serves 12–14.**

Creamed Spinach

2 (10-oz) packages frozen spinach, defrosted
4 tbsp unsalted butter
2 garlic cloves, pressed
1 shallot, finely chopped
1 cup half & half

½ tsp kosher salt
⅛ tsp ground white pepper
2 tbsp Parmigiano-Reggiano cheese, finely grated
Nutmeg, freshly grated, to taste

Place defrosted spinach in a clean dish towel and squeeze tightly to remove excess water. In a heavy suacepan, melt butter on medium heat. Add garlic and shallot. Sauté until glossy. Lower heat, add spinach and cook for about 3 minutes. Slowly add the half & half, a little bit at a time, until mixture thickens. Season with salt and pepper and continue cooking over medium low heat until all of the liquid has evaporated and mixture thickens. Stir in cheese and season with nutmeg. **Serves 4–6.**

Green Beans with Caramelized Onions

2 lb fresh green beans or hericots verts, ends trimmed
4 large yellow onions, ends removed, peeled and cut into thin wedges
6 tbsp unsalted butter, divided
½ tsp kosher salt
¼ tsp black pepper, freshly ground
1 tbsp granulated sugar
½ cup chicken broth, as needed
2 tbsp balsamic vinegar or red wine

In a heavy skillet, melt 4 tablespoons of butter over medium-high heat. Add onions and toss to coat well. Sprinkle with salt and pepper and reduce heat to medium low. Continue stirring onions and add sugar in small batches as onions slowly cook. Do not let the onions burn—only brown and then stir. Add chicken broth a tablespoon at a time, only as needed to keep onions moist.

After about 45 minutes, onions should be very brown, but not burnt. Add vinegar or wine to deglaze the pan at the very end just before removing onions.

Approximately 10 minutes before onions are finished cooking, place prepared green beans in a large pot of salted boiling water and cook for 5 minutes until crisp tender. Drain well and return to the same pot. Add remaining 2 tablespoons of butter and gently toss to coat. Place green beans on a large platter and top with caramelized onions. Serve immediately. **Serves 8.**

Thelma's Pie Crust

No offense to the turkey, but for me, Thanksgiving was and will always be about the pie. When I was little, holiday pie baking was a bustling, flour-dusted two-day collaboration between myself, my mother and close family friend Thelma. This foolproof, flaky recipe of Thelma's is still the only rolled crust recipe I use—it really does yield perfect results every time. Don't be intimidated by the thought of making your own crust! It's surprisingly easy, and it makes an incredible difference in the texture and flavor of your finished pie.

FOR 1 (10-INCH) PIE CRUST OR 1 (9-INCH) PIE CRUST WITH A LATTICE TOP:

2 cups all-purpose flour

3 tsp granulated sugar

½ tsp salt

½ cup Crisco

4 tbsp salted margarine

4–5 tbsp water, ice cold

FOR 1 (9-INCH) PIE CRUST ONLY:

1 ½ cups all-purpose flour

2 tsp granulated sugar

½ tsp salt

⅓ cup Crisco

3 tbsp salted margarine

2 ½ tbsp water, ice-cold

In a medium bowl, sift together the flour, sugar and salt. Cut in Crisco and margarine with pastry cutter or fork until it forms a coarse crumb. Add ice-cold water (I actually chill mine with ice cubes) 1 tablespoon at a time, adding only enough to hold the dough together. Mix until just combined. Flatten into disk on wax paper or plastic wrap and cover and chill in refrigerator for 20–30 minutes before use.

FOR PRE-BAKED PIE SHELL: Place rolled crust in pie plate and use a fork to poke holes all over. Bake at 400 degrees for 15 minutes. Let cool to room temperature before filling.

Thelma always used leftover crust dough to craft a special "baby pie" just for me—a tradition I now share with my daughter. If you find yourself without leftovers, you can always make a half-batch of Thelma's Pie Crust. You'll be glad you did.

Chocolate Pecan Pie

1 unbaked 10-inch pie crust

¼ cup unsalted butter

1 cup bittersweet chocolate chips

3 large eggs

1 cup granulated sugar

½ cup dark corn syrup

2 tsp pure vanilla extract

1 tsp pure chocolate extract (optional)

¼ tsp salt

1 cup raw pecan halves, plus extra for decorating the top

Preheat oven to 325 degrees. In a heavy saucepan over medium heat, melt together butter and chocolate. Set aside to cool slightly.

With electric mixer, beat eggs until foamy. Add sugar, corn syrup, vanilla extract, chocolate extract (if using) and salt.

Add cooled chocolate mixture to egg mixture and beat until well blended. Fold in nuts by hand. Pour into prepared pie crust and decorate top with pecans. Place pie on a rimmed baking sheet and bake for 45 minutes. **Serves 10.**

Pumpkin Chiffon Pie

This was a Grandma Jeanne classic! It is still the only pumpkin pie my family serves for Thanksgiving.

1 pre-baked 9-inch pie shell

1 (16-oz) can unsweetened pumpkin

1 ½ envelopes Knox® unflavored gelatin

⅔ cup (5 oz) evaporated milk

2 large eggs, separated

1 cup granulated sugar, divided

¼ tsp salt

1 tsp pure vanilla extract

½ tsp ground nutmeg

½ tsp ground ginger

⅛ tsp ground cloves

Fresh whipped cream for garnish

In a heavy saucepan, combine pumpkin, gelatin, milk, egg yolks, ⅔ cup of sugar, salt, vanilla and spices. Stir over low heat until gelatin dissolves and mixture is hot, but not boiling. Remove from heat and cool to room temperature. Cover and chill until mixture begins to thicken. Use an electric mixer to beat egg whites with remaining ⅓ cup of sugar until stiff peaks form. Gently fold beaten egg whites into chilled pumpkin mixture. Pour into prepared pie shell. Chill again for at least an hour. Serve with fresh whipped cream. **Serves 8.**

Apple Crumb Pie

1 unbaked 9-inch pie crust
4 Granny Smith apples, medium size
½ cup granulated sugar, unleveled
½ tsp ground cinnamon

1 tbsp all-purpose flour
2 tbsp unsalted butter, cut into small pieces
2 tbsp water
Crumb topping (recipe follows)

Preheat oven to 400 degrees. Peel and core the apples and slice very thinly. Set aside. In a small bowl, mix together the sugar, cinnamon and flour. Set aside. Sprinkle bottom of crust with a tablespoon of the dry ingredients and dot with several pieces of butter. Place apples in crust one layer at a time, sprinkle each layer with cinnamon/sugar mixture and dot with butter. Repeat until filled. Drizzle the water over apples. Sprinkle with crumb topping being sure to cover evenly. Place pie on rimmed baking sheet and bake for 40 minutes. If topping begins to brown too quickly, cover loosely with aluminum foil and continue baking. **Serves 8.**

Crumb Topping

⅓ cup salted butter or margarine   ½ cup granulated sugar   ¾ cup all-purpose flour

In a small bowl, blend all ingredients together with a fork until it forms a coarse crumb. Sprinkle evenly over pie filling.

Lemon Meringue Pie

1 (9-inch) graham cracker crust (recipe follows)
1 (14-oz) can Eagle Brand® sweetened condensed milk
½ cup lemon juice, freshly squeezed
2 tsp lemon zest
3 large eggs, divided
1 tsp lemon juice powder (optional, available online from the King Arthur Flour Co.)
¼ tsp cream of tartar
6 tbsp granulated sugar

Preheat oven to 325 degrees. In medium bowl, combine sweetened condensed milk, lemon juice, lemon zest, egg yolks and lemon juice powder if using. Blend until thickened. Pour into prepared crust.

Use an electric mixer to beat egg whites until foamy. Add cream of tartar, and gradually add the sugar one tablespoon at a time. Beat on highest speed until it becomes a shiny meringue.

Spread meringue over lemon filling, making sure to cover the edges of the pie. Place pie on rimmed baking sheet and bake for 12–15 minutes until top is golden brown. Cool pie completely and then refrigerate before serving. **Serves 8.**

Graham Cracker Crust

This easy, no-rolling-required crust is a great recipe to have on hand for those days when you prefer crumbly crust to flakey.

1 ½ cups fine graham cracker crumbs
¼ cup granulated sugar
½ cup unsalted butter or margarine, melted

Preheat oven to 375 degrees. In a small bowl, mix all ingredients together and press into ungreased 9-inch pie plate. Bake for 8 minutes and cool completely before filling. **Makes 1 (9-inch) pie crust.**

Bourbon Pecan Pie with Spice Crust

1 unbaked 9-inch spice crust (recipe follows)
3 large eggs
½ cup granulated sugar
½ cup dark corn syrup
4 tbsp unsalted butter, melted
⅛ cup bourbon
1 tsp pure vanilla extract
2 handfuls pecan pieces (use broken pieces for pie filling)
½ cup pecan halves, for decorating the top

Preheat oven to 350 degrees. Use an electric mixer to beat together all ingredients except pecans. Stir in pecan pieces by hand. Pour into prepared pie crust. Decorate top of pie with pecan halves, pressing gently to secure them. Place pie on rimmed baking sheet and bake for 50 minutes. **Serves 8.**

Spice Crust

1 cup all-purpose flour
¼ cup granulated sugar
¼ tsp salt
¼ tsp baking powder
¼ tsp ground cinnamon
⅛ tsp ground cloves
4 tbsp unsalted butter, cut into cubes
1 large egg yolk, beaten
1 tsp heavy cream

In a medium bowl, sift together flour, sugar, salt, baking powder, cinnamon and cloves. Add butter and use a fork or a pastry cutter to form a coarse crumb. Add egg and cream and mix until a soft, smooth dough forms. Place dough on wax paper or plastic wrap, press into disk and chill for at least one hour before use. **Makes 1 (9-inch) pie crust.**

Traditional Holiday Dinner

Every holiday meal has its traditional menu "staples"—and every family has additions and modifications that make the meal their own. Marriage invites yet another set of variations: a sweet little union of kitchens and cultures that will continue to evolve as children leave the nest to start families of their own.

The recipes in this section blend holiday favorites from my husband's family and my own, going back to our great-grandmothers and probably much further. Together, they represent the treasured dishes that have earned a permanent place on OUR family's table—edible heirlooms without which the celebration just wouldn't be complete. I hope some of them will earn a place on yours.

Starters
Mock Chopped Liver
Mushroom Rolls
Classic Chicken Soup with
    Homemade Kreplach

Side Dishes
Potato Pancakes with Fresh Applesauce
Deluxe Noodle Pudding (Kugel)
Spiced Carrot Ring with Peas

Main Courses
Tender Beef Brisket with Roasted Root Vegetables
Sweet & Sour Stuffed Cabbage

Desserts
Hannah's Lemon Cake
Poppyseed Crisps (Mun Cookies)
Rugelach
Little Snails (Schnecken)
Blackberry Jam-Filled Cookies
Chocolate Chip Rum Cake

Mock Chopped Liver

½ large yellow onion, chopped

2 tbsp extra-virgin olive oil

1 lb fresh green string beans, ends trimmed,
    cooked until crisp tender

1 hard-boiled egg, chopped

½ cup walnuts, ground

Kosher salt, to taste

Black pepper, freshly ground to taste

¼ small onion, grated

In a sauté pan, cook onions in oil until lightly browned. Set aside to cool. Grind together cooked onions, green beans, egg and walnuts in a food processor. Season with salt and pepper. Fold grated raw onion into ground mixture, cover and chill overnight so that flavors will be well blended. Serve with crackers or toast points. **Serves 8.**

Mushroom Rolls

18 slices white bread, crusts removed

6 tbsp unsalted butter or margarine, divided

1 yellow onion

1 lb fresh white button mushrooms, cleaned

½ tsp salt

¼ tsp ground white pepper

1 tsp dried mushroom powder (optional)

3 tsp Maggi Liquid Seasoning

½ tsp granulated sugar

2 tbsp all-purpose flour, as needed

On a wooden board, roll each slice of bread with rolling pin until very thin and flat. Set aside. In medium sauté pan, warm 4 tablespoons of butter or margarine over low heat until melted. In food processor, finely chop onion and add to melted butter. Sauté on medium heat for a few minutes until onions are glossy and soft.

Finely chop mushrooms in food processor and add to onions. Stir in salt, pepper, mushroom powder, Maggi Seasoning and sugar. Continue to cook over medium heat about 10 minutes, stirring constantly. Add flour as needed to thicken mixture until it reaches spreading consistency. Continue to cook for another 3–5 minutes.

Cool mixture to room temperature. Spread each piece of bread with a layer of mushroom filling. Roll up tightly, jelly roll style. Cover and place in refrigerator for 1 hour. When ready to serve, adjust oven rack to top position and set oven temperature to broil. Melt remaining 2 tablespoons of butter or margarine. Cut each roll in half and trim off uneven edges. Brush each roll with melted butter or margarine. Place on broiling pan and broil until golden brown on top. Serve immediately. **Makes 36 rolls.**

Classic Chicken Soup with Homemade Kreplach

This rich, clear, flavorful classic from Grandma Jeanne contains *kreplach*—the Yiddish word for dumpling. These savory, meat-filled pockets elevate an everyday favorite to a special starter that's perfect for any occasion. Cousin to the wonton, empanada and tortellini, kreplach are proof positive that dumplings are delicious in any language.

4 Kosher split chicken breasts, skin, rib meat and bones attached
6 (14.5-oz) cans or 3 (32-oz) boxes Swanson® Fat-Free Chicken Broth
2 tsp chicken base (I like Better than Bouillon®)
6 fresh carrots, peeled and cut in half
6 fresh celery stalks, cleaned
3 yellow onions, quartered
1 to 2 bunches fresh parsley root, peeled, stems and leaves attached
Kreplach (recipe follows)
Fresh dill, to garnish

Wash chicken breasts with cold water. Pat dry with paper towels. Place chicken in stock pot and cover until ¾ full with chicken broth. Bring to a boil, continually skimming foam and fat with fine-mesh skimmer.

When all of the foam and fat has been removed, stir in chicken base to taste. Add carrots, celery, onions and parsley root and begin to boil lightly to blend flavors. Reduce heat and cover. Simmer over a low flame for at least 3 hours.

Remove chicken and vegetables from broth. Reserve carrots, celery and chicken to cut when cool. Remove skin and bones from chicken and discard. Cut meat into cubes, place in container and refrigerate. Slice carrots and celery and place in separate containers to refrigerate. Cool, skim and strain soup through a fine-mesh sieve and place clear broth in large glass bowl. Place a piece of plastic wrap directly on top of soup so that congealed fat will stick to it after refrigeration. Refrigerate soup overnight. Remove plastic wrap with fat and skim once more before reheating.

To serve, place desired amount of broth into pot. Heat at medium high heat until soup is very hot. Add either kreplach or chicken, sliced carrots and celery. Ladle into soup bowls and garnish with fresh dill to serve. **Serves 10.**

Kreplach

FOR THE DOUGH:
1 large egg
2 tbsp vegetable oil
¼ tsp salt
2 tbsp water
1 cup all-purpose flour
½ tsp baking powder

FOR THE FILLING:
½ lb chicken or beef, cooked and ground
¼ cup yellow onion, grated
Salt, to taste
Black pepper, freshly ground to taste
1 large egg, beaten

FOR THE DOUGH: In a medium bowl, use a fork to beat egg slightly. Add the remaining ingredients until dough becomes soft and smooth. Let stand covered at room temperature for at least one hour or longer for easier handling.

FOR THE FILLING: Mix together chicken or beef, onion, salt and pepper. Add egg and mix until filling holds together. Set aside.

On a lightly floured board, roll out dough very thin and cut into strips. (Do not use too much flour, or the dough will become dry and will not stay pinched together.)

Cut strips into small squares (approximately 2 inches) and place a spoonful of filling in the center of each square. Fold in half to form triangle and press edges firmly to seal. Trim edges with a sharp knife, being careful not to cut the seal. Bring two ends of the triangle together and pinch firmly to join. Place kreplach in a large pot of salted water set to medium-high heat. Cook UNCOVERED for 20–25 minutes. Drain well. Serve in homemade chicken soup instead of noodles or matzoh balls. **Makes approximately 24 kreplach.**

Potato Pancakes with Fresh Applesauce

6 Yukon Gold potatoes, peeled

1 yellow onion, chopped

2 large eggs

Pinch baking powder

Pinch kosher salt

Pinch black pepper, freshly ground

Pinch ground white pepper

All-purpose flour, as needed

Matzo meal, as needed

Vegetable oil, for frying

Fresh applesauce (recipe follows)

Sour cream, for garnish

Grind potatoes, onion, eggs, baking powder, salt and peppers together in a food processor. Add just enough matzo meal and flour to bind. The consistency should be slightly thicker than pancake batter.

In a heavy skillet, heat vegetable oil on medium heat. Using ¼ cup scoop as a guideline for size, form small, thin pancakes with hands. With slotted spoon, ladle pancakes into skillet and fry until golden brown, being sure to flip over halfway through to evenly brown both sides. Drain on paper towels and serve warm with fresh applesauce and sour cream. **Makes approximately 18 pancakes.**

Applesauce

While this is THE classic companion to potato pancakes, homemade applesauce is wonderful on its own, too! I've found that blending McIntosh and Golden Delicious apples creates a lovely depth of flavor—but any apple that softens easily when cooked will work. Remember that you may need to adjust the amount of water and sugar for different varieties.

10 fresh apples, peeled, cored and cut into chunks

1 cup water, scant

¾ cup granulated sugar

1 tbsp lemon juice, freshly squeezed

1 tsp ground cinnamon, or more to taste

Place apples in a large pot. Add water, sugar and lemon juice. Cook uncovered over low to medium-low heat, stirring occasionally until soft. Mash with potato masher and continue cooking. Add cinnamon to taste. If apples are not mashing easily, lower heat and cook covered for a few additional minutes. **Makes 4 cups.**

Deluxe Noodle Pudding (Kugel)

1 lb wide egg noodles
1 lb cottage cheese, small curd
16 oz sour cream
1 cup whole milk
8 tbsp unsalted butter, melted
½ cup granulated sugar
4 large eggs, beaten
1 tsp pure vanilla extract

½ tsp salt
½ cup golden raisins (optional)
1 cup corn flakes cereal
    (crushed before measuring)
1 tsp ground cinnamon
¼ cup brown sugar, firmly packed
½ cup apples, thinly sliced (optional)

Preheat oven to 350 degrees. Butter a 9x13 baking dish. Cook noodles according to directions on package. Drain well. In large bowl, use a rubber spatula to mix together the cottage cheese, sour cream, milk, butter, sugar, eggs, vanilla and salt. Add raisins if using. Toss with noodles until evenly coated. Transfer to prepared baking dish.

NOTE: If using apples, slice apples very thinly and layer in middle of casserole by filling half of the baking dish with noodles, layering apples on top, and then placing remaining noodles on top of apple layer.

Mix together the corn flakes, cinnamon and brown sugar. Sprinkle evenly over top of noodles. Bake for 1–1 ½ hours. The pudding should be set, but not too brown. **Serves 14.**

Spiced Carrot Ring with Peas

½ cup butter or margarine
2 large eggs, separated
⅓ cup dark brown sugar, firmly packed
2 tsp lemon juice, freshly squeezed
1 tsp pure vanilla extract
2 (4-oz) jars puréed unsweetened baby food carrots
½ tsp ground cinnamon

Pinch ground nutmeg
1 ¼ cups sifted all-purpose flour
    (sift before measuring)
½ tsp baking powder
½ tsp baking soda
¼ tsp salt

Preheat oven to 350 degrees. Grease a 6-cup ring mold. Use an electric mixer to cream together butter or margarine, egg yolks, brown sugar, lemon juice, vanilla, carrots, cinnamon and nutmeg. Fold in dry ingredients by hand.

Use an electric mixer to beat egg whites until stiff peaks form. Gently fold egg whites into carrot mixture. Pour into prepared ring and bake for 20 minutes. To serve, unmold and fill center with cooked peas or a combination of peas and carrots. **Serves 12–14.**

Tender Beef Brisket

The best brisket begins with the best cut of meat. I only use the center cut, and I always trim off all of the fat before I begin.

1 (3–5 lb) center-cut beef brisket, trimmed of all fat
Lawry's Seasoned Salt, to taste
Onion powder, to taste
Garlic powder, to taste
1 (20-oz) bottle barbecue sauce without smoke flavoring (I use Famous Dave's® Rich
    & Sassy Original Recipe)
1 ½ cups water
3 yellow onions, quartered

Turn oven to broil setting but leave oven rack in middle position. Place trimmed meat in a large roasting pan and lightly season on both sides with seasoned salt, onion powder and garlic powder. Broil meat for 5 minutes on each side until it is lightly browned. Remove from oven and reduce temperature to 325 degrees. In a small bowl, mix the barbecue sauce with water and pour over browned meat. Add onions and cover with foil. Return to oven to bake for 4 hours, turning meat over once after 2 hours. Be sure to check the amount of liquid halfway through baking—if the sauce looks too thick, add a little bit more water.

When finished cooking, remove brisket from sauce and place on large cutting board. Use a slotted spoon to remove most of the onions, but reserve all of the liquid in the roasting pan. With a sharp knife (or electric knife, if you have one) slice meat across the grain. Place sliced brisket back in the pan with sauce.

Let cool to room temperature, then cover and refrigerate. Before serving, reheat covered at 250 degrees for 30 minutes. Serve with roasted root vegetables (recipe follows). **Serves 6–8.**

Roasted Root Vegetables

1 lb fresh carrots, peeled and tops removed
1 lb fresh parsnips, peeled and tops removed
⅓ cup extra-virgin olive oil

Salt, to taste
Black pepper, freshly ground to taste
1 small bunch fresh dill, for garnish

Preheat oven to 400 degrees. Slice carrots and parsnip in half lengthwise and then again into quarters. Place oil in a large bowl. Add vegetables and toss to coat evenly. Season with salt and pepper to taste. Place on rimmed baking sheet and roast for 20 minutes. With a metal spatula, toss and turn once and continue roasting for another 20–25 minutes until edges begin to crisp and brown. Sprinkle liberally with fresh snipped dill before serving. **Serves 8–10.**

Sweet & Sour Stuffed Cabbage

1 head green cabbage (NOT savoy cabbage)

1 lb ground beef

¼ cup white rice, cooked in ½ cup water (NOT instant rice)

1 large egg

4 tbsp unsalted butter

1 yellow onion, diced

2 cups canned tomato sauce

⅛ cup lemon juice, freshly squeezed

⅛ cup white vinegar

¼ cup brown sugar, firmly packed

¼ tsp salt

¾–1 cup water, as needed

Place whole cabbage in plastic bag in the freezer for 2 days and then defrost in the refrigerator overnight. The leaves will easily come apart; this prevents you having to cook them.

Preheat oven to 350 degrees. In a medium bowl, combine ground beef, cooked rice and egg. Mix well and set aside. In a small sauté pan, melt butter over medium heat. Add onions and sauté until golden brown. Add half of the cooked onions to the meat mixture and stir to combine.

Place a ball of meat mixture in the center of each cabbage leaf and roll up, tucking the ends securely. Place close together in a 9x13 roasting pan. Combine remaining cooked onions with tomato sauce, lemon juice, vinegar, brown sugar and salt and pour over top of cabbage rolls. Add only enough water so that sauce covers the rolls. Cover with aluminum foil and bake for 1 ½ hours, removing the cover for the last 20 minutes of baking. **Makes 12 cabbage rolls.**

The mercury glass globes pictured here are Victorian butler's balls. They enabled one's servants to stand at an unobtrusive distance with a full view of the table, and thus seem to magically anticipate guests' every need. Although we don't have a butler, our guests do enjoy trying to guess what they are… and the name always gets a laugh.

Hannah's Lemon Cake

This simple, super-moist and lemony sheet cake recipe came from my Grandmother Hannah. It tastes even better on the second or third day, so it's great for making ahead (or having for breakfast). Full disclosure: I have never served this cake without being asked for the recipe, so I must come clean about my love for box cakes. There's no shame here—after all, they are the only cakes that I know that will always love me back.

1 box Duncan Hines® Yellow Cake mix
1 (3.4-oz) box vanilla instant pudding mix
1 ½ cups orange juice, freshly squeezed and divided
4 large eggs
⅔ cup vegetable oil
¾ cup granulated sugar
¼ cup lemon juice, freshly squeezed

Preheat oven to 325 degrees. Grease a 9x13 baking pan. I prefer to use one that is NOT non-stick or coated. If you can find a cake pan with a removable bottom, it gives you the option of serving the cake whole rather than serving it in the pan or having to pre-cut before plating.

Using an electric mixer, beat together the cake mix, pudding mix, 1 cup orange juice, eggs and oil until batter is smooth and very few lumps remain. Pour into prepared pan and bake for 50 minutes. Ten minutes before cake has finished baking, combine the sugar, remaining ½ cup orange juice and lemon juice in a small saucepan. Lightly boil the mixture and then reduce heat, stirring constantly until sugar is dissolved. Set aside.

When cake comes out of the oven, immediately poke holes over the entire top of the cake using a large two-pronged fork. Spoon warm liquid topping over cake. Let cake cool completely, leave in the pan and cover with aluminum foil. Wait 1 day before serving. **Serves 16.**

Poppyseed Crisps (Mun Cookies)

This lost recipe from my husband's grandmother Dorothy was THE family favorite. Poppyseed—or *Mun,* which is Yiddish for poppyseed—Crisps sustained the brood throughout their childhood, arriving at summer camps and college dorms in coffee can care packages. After many years and many failed attempts, we were finally able to recreate Grandma Dorothy's amazing signature sweet.

1 cup granulated sugar

2 large eggs, room temperature

¾ cup vegetable oil

2 tsp pure vanilla extract

2 tsp water

½ cup poppy seeds

2 cups all-purpose flour

Pinch salt

Pinch baking soda

Preheat oven to 350 degrees. Line baking sheets with parchment paper and lightly grease paper. Using an electric mixer, beat sugar, eggs, oil and vanilla on medium speed until well blended. Add water and poppy seeds and mix a minute longer. Slowly add flour, salt and baking soda mixing until just combined. Cover and refrigerate dough for at least one hour or until thoroughly chilled and cold enough to handle.

Lightly flour hands and roll dough into teaspoon-sized balls. Place on cookie sheet approximately 2 inches apart. Use lightly floured fingertips to flatten dough until almost paper thin. Bake for 10 minutes or until edges become golden brown and cookies begin to crisp. Gently remove with spatula and cool on wire rack. These cookies will keep for 2 weeks in an airtight container. **Makes approximately 48 cookies.**

Rugelach

FOR THE DOUGH:
8 oz cream cheese, room temperature
8 oz unsalted butter, room temperature
⅛ cup confectioner's sugar
2 tsp pure vanilla extract
2 cups all-purpose flour
½ tsp baking powder

FOR THE TOPPING:
2 egg yolks, room temperature
1 tbsp heavy cream
Premixed sugar/cinnamon,
    for sprinkling

FOR THE FILLING:
⅓ cup brown sugar, firmly packed
6 tbsp granulated sugar
1 tsp ground cinnamon
1 cup golden raisins
1 cup walnuts, finely ground (optional)
1 cup apricot preserves, puréed in food processor or blender

FOR THE DOUGH: Use an electric mixer to cream together cream cheese and butter until blended. Add sugar and vanilla and continue to blend. Add flour and baking powder, and mix until just combined. Place dough onto lightly floured wax paper and roll into ball. Cut ball into quarters (I weigh them to ensure they are equal in size) and flatten each quarter into disk shape. Wrap in plastic and refrigerate for at least 1 hour.

FOR THE FILLING: In a small bowl, combine the sugars, cinnamon, raisins and walnuts (if using). Set aside.

Preheat oven to 350 degrees. Line baking sheets with parchment paper. On a well-floured board, roll out each disk into a 9-inch circle. Spread the dough with a thin layer of preserves and sprinkle with ½ cup of the filling.

Press filling lightly into dough. Cut the circle into 16 equal wedges—first cutting the circle in half, and then each half into 8 wedges. Be sure that the raisins are evenly distributed so that each roll will have some. Starting with the wide, outside edge, tightly roll up each wedge into a crescent, tucking as you go. Place rugelach on prepared baking sheet. Chill for 30 minutes.

FOR THE TOPPING: In a small bowl, whisk together egg yolks and cream. Lightly brush each rugelach with the egg wash and sprinkle tops with cinnamon/sugar mixture. Bake for 25 minutes, until rugelach are lightly browned. Remove to a wire rack and cool. **Makes 64 rugelach.**

Little Snails (Schnecken)

A Jewish holiday tradition that absolutely everyone loves—SO amazing when served piping hot, right out of the oven!

FOR THE DOUGH:
4 ½ tsp SAF® Brand instant yeast* (available online)
4 large eggs, room temperature
1 cup sour cream
8 oz unsalted butter, melted and cooled
¼ cup granulated sugar
2 tsp pure vanilla extract
½ tsp salt
4 cups all-purpose flour

FOR THE FILLING:
½ cup unsalted butter, melted
1 cup brown sugar, firmly packed
1 tbsp pure vanilla extract
1 tbsp ground cinnamon
2 cups golden raisins
¼ lb pecan pieces, lightly toasted

FOR THE DOUGH: Using an electric mixer, combine yeast, eggs, sour cream, butter, sugar, vanilla and salt. Mix thoroughly. Gradually add the flour and mix until just combined. Place dough in large glass bowl and cover with paper towel. Place in refrigerator for 4 hours or overnight for slow cold rise in order to bake them fresh for breakfast.

FOR THE FILLING: In a small bowl, combine the butter, sugar, vanilla and cinnamon. Set aside.

When dough has doubled in size, remove from refrigerator and divide into thirds. Prepare each muffin cup with 1 teaspoon of filling and drop in a few chopped pecans. (You can always mix up more of this if you run short.) Be sure that you DO NOT use a non-stick muffin tins.

Preheat oven to 325 degrees. Knead each section until dough is smooth and elastic. On a well-floured board, roll out dough into rectangle one section at a time. Spread ⅓ of the filling mixture generously on each rectangle. Sprinkle raisins over sugar mixture and roll up dough jelly roll-style, carefully tucking in the raisins and filling as you go. Using a sharp knife, slice dough log into 12 equal parts and place in prepared muffin cups cut-side down. Place pan over warm stove or oven and cover with dish towel until rolls double in size.

Bake for 15–20 minutes until slightly browned. Immediately invert onto waxed paper to cool. **Makes 36 schnecken.**

*With instant yeast, there is no need to proof first—it is simply added with the other ingredients.

Blackberry Jam-Filled Cookies

¼ cup salted margarine

¼ cup Crisco

¼ cup sifted confectioner's sugar (sift before measuring)

½ tsp pure vanilla extract

1 cup sifted all-purpose flour (sift before measuring)

1 (12-oz) jar seedless blackberry jam

Preheat oven to 350 degrees. Lightly flour an ungreased baking sheet. In a medium bowl, use a wooden spoon to cream together margarine, Crisco, sugar and vanilla. Add flour and blend until a soft dough forms. Cover dough and let rest for 30 minutes at room temperature for easier handling.

Dust hands with flour and roll dough into cherry-sized balls. Place balls on prepared baking sheet and make a well in the center of each ball by gently pressing centers with a finger dipped in flour. Spoon a small drop of jam in each center. Be careful to only use a tiny amount of jam to avoid running when baking.

Bake for approximately 10–12 minutes but watch carefully and remove when edges just begin to brown slightly. While cookies are hot, immediately fill the centers of each cookie with reserved jam. Allow cookies to cool to room temperature for jam to set. **Makes 18 cookies.**

Chocolate Chip Rum Cake

I'll admit that I'm usually the last person to reach for a slice of "liquor cake," but somehow the rum in this old-school confection cuts the sweetness to perfection.

1 box Duncan Hines Classic Butter Golden Cake Mix

1 (3.4-oz) box vanilla instant pudding mix

4 oz unsalted butter, room temperature

4 large eggs, room temperature

8 oz sour cream, room temperature

½ cup vegetable oil

4 tsp pure vanilla extract

4 tbsp white rum

6 oz semi-sweet chocolate chips

1 cup walnuts, chopped (optional)

Preheat oven to 325 degrees. Generously grease a 12-cup bundt pan. Do NOT use a dark-coated non-stick pan for this cake. Instead, use an aluminum bundt pan (such as a Nordic Ware® The Original 12-cup Bundt Pan, available online).

Using an electric mixer, beat all of the ingredients together EXCEPT for chocolate chips (and nuts if you're using them) at medium-high speed for 3–5 minutes. Batter should be smooth and thick.

Fold in chocolate chips (and nuts if you're using them) by hand. Pour into prepared bundt pan and bake for 1 hour. Check with cake tester at 50 minutes. Let cool for 30 minutes before unmolding. **Serves 16.**

New Year's Eve

I don't recall exactly when we began the tradition of celebrating this night at home, but every year I am reminded that there is no place I would rather be than here, in the company of family and good friends. We laugh together about times past, look forward to days ahead and toast the coming year with hearts full of happiness and hope.

It is also the one night of the year that is all *gilt* and no *guilt*. Happily adopting a "more is more" mindset, we set our table with everything old and gold—then lay out a decadent buffet dinner brimming with opulent drinks, rich foods and indulgent desserts. But although the table is our most formal of the year, we always manage to keep the vibe casual and fun. No matter where and how you and yours choose to celebrate, this is the magic the evening offers: to gather with those closest to you, and to bask together in the glittering promise of a new beginning.

Cocktails

Rosé Champagne with Elderflower

Death in the Afternoon Cocktail

Hors d'oeuvres

Mini Crab Cakes with Lemon Pepper Remoulade

Mushroom Soup

Warm Brie Tarts with Truffled Honey Drizzle

Buffet

Hearts of Butter Lettuce with Honey Mustard Dressing

Gruyère Cheese Gougères

Marinated Whole Beef Tenderloin

Coq au Vin

Spinach Rockefeller

Potato Casserole

Dessert

Chilled Raspberry Mousse

Warm Apple Tarts

More is More Chocolate
Soufflé Tart

Rosé Champagne with Elderflower

1 (750-ml) bottle rosé champagne, very well chilled
1 (200-ml) bottle St. Germain (elderflower liqueur)
Granulated sugar, to garnish rim
Gold dust powder, to garnish rim (available online)

Dip the rims of 6 champagne flutes into a small bowl of water. Next, dip each wet rim into a small bowl of granulated sugar and then into a small bowl of gold dust powder. Pour 1.5 oz of St. Germain into each of the flutes. Top with 4.5 oz of very well chilled rosé champagne. Serve immediately. **Serves 6.**

Death in the Afternoon Cocktail

Ernest Hemingway invented this absinthe and champagne cocktail, and, like his prose, it gets straight to the point. I've always assumed it was named for the way you feel the next day if you have more than one, but I haven't personally tested this theory. New Year's Eve does seem like the perfect time to try.

1 (750-ml) bottle absinthe
1 (750-ml) bottle champagne, very well chilled

To each glass, first add 1.5 oz absinthe, then top with 4.5 oz of chilled champagne. Serve immediately.
Serves 6.

Mini Crab Cakes
with Lemon Pepper Remoulade

1–2 lb Maryland jumbo lump crab meat

1 large egg

½ cup mayonnaise

2 tbsp whole-grain mustard

1 tbsp lemon juice, freshly squeezed

¾ tsp Lawry's Seasoned Salt or Old Bay® Seasoning

½ tsp ground white pepper

½ cup fresh parsley, chopped

1–2 fresh scallions, chopped

¼ red bell pepper, seeds and ribs removed, finely diced

¼ cup seasoned bread crumbs

Lemon Pepper Remoulade (recipe follows)

Preheat oven to 400 degrees. Lightly oil a baking sheet. Place crab meat in a medium bowl and pick over to remove cartilage, being careful not to break up lumps. In a separate large bowl, whisk the egg until frothy. Add mayonnaise, mustard, lemon juice, seasoned salt and pepper and whisk until smooth. Add parsley, scallions and bell pepper and mix well. Fold in the crab meat and add the bread crumbs, gently mixing until just combined. Form crab mixture into cakes that are 2 inches in diameter and 1 inch thick. Place on prepared baking sheet and bake for 15 minutes or until lightly golden, turning with a metal spatula once or twice during baking so the cakes do not stick. Serve warm over mixed field greens with lemon pepper remoulade (recipe follows).

NOTE: You can make these several hours ahead and reheat immediately prior to serving. After baking, cool, cover and chill. Just before serving, preheat the broiler. Broil crab cakes 1–2 minutes on each side, just to heat through. Remove from broiler, cover loosely with aluminum foil and let stand 3 minutes before serving. **Makes 24 crab cakes.**

Lemon Pepper Remoulade

⅓ cup cornichons, well drained

1 tsp cornichon juice

¼ cup capers, well drained

1 large shallot, peeled and chopped

1 ½ cups mayonnaise

1 tsp lemon juice, freshly squeezed

1 tbsp lemon zest

1 tbsp brandy

¼ cup fresh chives, chopped

1 tbsp black pepper, coarsely ground

¼ tsp cayenne pepper

In the bowl of a food processor fitted with a metal blade, combine cornichons, cornichon juice, capers and shallot and pulse until finely minced. Transfer to a small bowl and blend in all remaining ingredients. Cover and chill overnight to allow flavors to blend before serving. **Makes 2 cups.**

Mushroom Soup

This full-bodied soup has a creamy consistency, without cream—although it does have a touch of butter. I serve this soup in demitasse cups as an appetizer, but it also makes a hearty meal when served in a large bowl with some crusty fresh-baked bread.

2 tbsp unsalted butter

1 cup fresh carrots, peeled and sliced

½ cup fresh celery, chopped

1 cup yellow onion, sliced

1 cup fresh leeks, sliced, white and light green
      parts only

2 lb fresh white button mushrooms, cleaned and sliced

1 tsp fresh thyme leaves, chopped

6 cups chicken broth

1 ½ tsp salt

⅛ tsp black pepper, freshly ground

Fresh chives or fresh chive blossoms
      for garnish

Truffle oil, for garnish (optional)

In a large pot, melt butter over medium heat. Add carrots, celery, onions and leeks. Cover and cook until tender, but not browned. Let vegetables sweat in pot, stirring occasionally, for 10–15 minutes. Stir in mushrooms and thyme, and cook until tender and soft. Add chicken broth, salt and pepper and simmer covered for 45 minutes. Let soup cool almost to room temperature and purée in a food processor or blender until velvety smooth. To serve, heat soup until very hot, sprinkle with a dash of fresh chopped chives or chive blossom, and garnish with a drizzle of truffle oil. **Serves 12–14.**

Warm Brie Tarts with Truffled Honey Drizzle

The delicate combination of flavors makes this a wonderful hors d'oeuvre. If white truffles are in season and you are in the mood to splurge, purchase a tiny amount and shave paper-thin slices over the top of each tart.

24 mini pre-baked neutral tart shells

1 lb triple-crème Brie cheese, very cold

½ cup honey (or truffle-infused honey), to drizzle

White truffle oil, to drizzle

Preheat oven to 250 degrees. Line rimmed baking sheet with parchment paper and place 24 mini tart shells on top. Drizzle the inside of each shell with honey. Using a sharp knife, remove rind from cheese and divide into 24 small chunks or cubes, just large enough to fill the tart when it melts. Place cheese in prepared shell and bake only until cheese melts, approximately 5 minutes. While tarts are warm, drizzle tops with honey and truffle oil. Serve immediately. **Makes 24 tarts.**

Hearts of Butter Lettuce with Honey Mustard Dressing

2 heads butter lettuce

2 tbsp apple cider vinegar

2 tbsp honey

3 tbsp mayonnaise

2 tsp Dijon mustard

1 ½ tsp fresh shallot, minced

½ tbsp fresh parsley, minced

⅛ tsp salt

1 cup vegetable oil

Cut each lettuce head into 4 wedges. In a small saucepan over low heat, warm vinegar and honey together until honey melts. Pour into a glass bowl to cool. Whisk in mayonnaise, mustard, shallot, parsley and salt until blended. Gradually add oil in steady stream while whisking until emulsified. Drizzle over lettuce wedges. **Serves 8.**

Gruyère Cheese Gougères

6 tbsp unsalted butter
1 cup water
½ tsp salt
1 ½ cups bread flour
Pinch cayenne pepper
6 large eggs, room temperature
2 cups fresh Gruyère cheese, coarsely grated and divided
2 tbsp Parmigiano-Reggiano cheese, freshly grated

Preheat oven to 400 degrees. Line baking sheets with parchment paper. In medium saucepan, combine the butter, water and salt. Bring to a light boil and remove from heat. Using a wooden spoon, stir in the flour and the cayenne pepper. Add eggs to flour mixture one at a time, stirring well after each addition, until fully incorporated into a smooth dough. Stir in 1 ½ cups of the Gruyère cheese and the Parmigiano-Reggiano cheese. Scoop heaping tablespoons of dough onto prepared baking sheets. Space them at least 3 inches apart to allow room to puff when baking. Sprinkle tops with remaining ½ cup of Gruyère cheese. Bake for 25 minutes, until balls puff and become golden. Serve immediately or cool completely on wire rack and reheat in 200 degree oven immediately before serving. **Makes approxiately 12 gougères.**

Marinated Whole Beef Tenderloin

1 whole center-cut prime beef tenderloin (approximately 4 lb, all fat trimmed)
¾ cup soy sauce
¼ cup sesame oil
¼ cup all-purpose flour
¼ cup granulated sugar
¼ cup toasted sesame seeds
4 fresh green onions, chopped
2 fresh garlic cloves, chopped
¼ tsp crushed red pepper flakes

Place prepared beef in a large Ziploc bag. In a medium bowl, mix all remaining ingredients together and pour over beef. Seal bag and chill 6 hours or overnight to blend flavors.

Move oven rack to second-highest from top and set oven to broil. Place meat in the center of a slotted broiling pan and broil for 10 minutes on each side. When meat is well browned on both sides, remove from oven. Adjust rack to center position and reduce oven temperature to 375 degrees. Return meat to oven, close door and cook for another 15 minutes. Let meat sit for at least 5 minutes before slicing, as it will continue to cook while it sits on the pan. **Serves 8.**

Coq au Vin

3 lb chicken, skin and bones attached (I prefer to
    use all breasts, but you may use thighs too)
½ cup all-purpose flour
1 ½ tsp salt, divided
¼ tsp black pepper, freshly ground
6 slices uncooked bacon, thick center cut
8 oz fresh white button mushrooms, washed,
    dried and sliced
6 small onions, sliced

1 bay leaf
½ tsp dried thyme
2 fresh carrots, julienned
2 chicken bouillon cubes
1 cup water, hot
1 cup Burgundy wine
1 garlic clove, crushed
2 fresh parsley sprigs

Wash chicken and pat dry with paper towel. In a medium bowl, mix together flour, 1 teaspoon salt
and pepper. Coat chicken with flour mixture and set aside. In a large skillet, cook bacon until crisp.
Remove bacon, drain on paper towel and leave bacon fat in skillet. Add chicken to skillet, starting
with skin side down and brown on both sides. Remove from skillet and set aside. Add mushrooms
and onions to skillet and stir until slightly browned. Crumble bacon and add to skillet. Add bay leaf,
thyme, carrots, bouillon, water, wine, garlic, parsley and remaining ½ teaspoon salt and mix well.
Add browned chicken and cover. Simmer for 1 hour over low heat. **Serves 6.**

Spinach Rockefeller

6–8 thick slices fresh tomato (or 6 to 8 small tomatoes, scooped out)

2 (10-oz) packages frozen chopped spinach

¼ cup plain bread crumbs

¼ cup fresh scallions, minced

2 large eggs, lightly beaten

2 tbsp unsalted butter, melted and slightly cooled

¼ cup Parmigiano-Reggiano cheese, freshly grated

½ tsp fresh garlic, minced

½ tsp fresh thyme, minced

⅛ tsp black pepper, freshly ground

¼ tsp salt

Garlic salt, to taste

Preheat oven to 350 degrees. Cook spinach according to package instructions. Drain by placing chopped spinach in a clean dish towel and squeeze tightly to remove excess water. In a medium bowl, combine spinach, bread crumbs, scallions, eggs, butter, cheese, garlic, thyme, pepper and salt. Blend well. Arrange tomato slices (or scooped whole tomatoes) in a single layer in a shallow baking dish. Sprinkle tomatoes with garlic salt and spoon ¼ cup of the spinach mixture onto each tomato slice or into each scooped tomato. Bake uncovered for 15 minutes or until set and thoroughly heated. **Serves 6–8.**

Potato Casserole

1 (24-oz) package frozen shredded potatoes

1 cup half & half

¼ cup unsalted butter or margarine

1 tbsp dried minced onion flakes

2 tsp caraway seeds

1 tsp salt

½ tsp ground white pepper

½ cup Parmigiano-Reggiano cheese, freshly grated

Preheat oven to 350 degrees. Grease a shallow casserole dish (I use a 10-inch round glass one). Thaw potatoes. In a medium saucepan, bring the half & half to a boil. Reduce heat, add the potatoes and stir until liquid is absorbed. Add butter and gently stir with spatula until melted. Stir in the onion, caraway seeds, salt and pepper. Adjust seasonings to taste. Spoon potato mixture into prepared dish. Sprinkle with cheese. Bake for one hour or until top is brown and bubbly. **Serves 6–8.**

Chilled Raspberry Mousse

This cool, creamy dessert may seem a bit summery, but it has become a year-round favorite in our home.

6 oz fresh raspberries
¾ cup granulated sugar, divided, plus 2 tbsp
4 large eggs, separated
Pinch salt
1 tbsp unflavored gelatin
¼ cup cold water
1 cup heavy cream, whipped

Prepare 1-quart soufflé dish: fold a 21-inch piece of wax paper into thirds lengthwise and brush one side with oil. Wrap paper around the dish, oiled side facing inward, to form a 3-inch-high collar. Secure with tape.

Purée raspberries in blender. Transfer purée to medium bowl and sprinkle with 2 tablespoons of sugar. Set aside to allow sugar to dissolve. In medium saucepan, whisk together egg yolks, ½ cup of sugar and pinch of salt. Cook over medium-low heat, whisking constantly until mixture thickens like custard. Do not boil, or custard will curdle. Remove from heat and let cool for 10 minutes.

Sprinkle the unflavored gelatin over cold water to soften slightly. Add gelatin mixture to cooled custard and whisk to combine. Add raspberry purée and whisk again until well blended. Chill raspberry custard mixture in refrigerator until thickened—about 20 minutes.

Using an electric mixer, beat the cup of heavy cream until light and fluffy. Set aside. Next, use the electric mixer to beat the egg whites until foamy. Gradually add the remaining ¼ cup of sugar and beat on highest speed to make a shiny meringue. Remove raspberry custard from refrigerator and alternately fold meringue with whipped cream into raspberry custard. Pour mixture into prepared dish and refrigerate several hours or overnight. Remove collar prior to serving. **Serves 6–8.**

NOTE: This mousse may also be served in individual dessert glasses, as pictured.

Warm Apple Tarts

This recipe came from a cooking class given by Jean-Pierre at his eponymous Palm Beach bistro. These authentic French apple tarts are wonderfully delicate, crisp and delicious—they make an impressive presentation, but they are incredibly uncomplicated to make.

2 sheets frozen puff pastry, defrosted
3 Golden Delicious apples, peeled, halved, cored and cut into thin slices
1 cup homemade applesauce (see recipe on page 177)
2 tbsp unsalted butter, melted
3 tbsp granulated sugar

Preheat oven to 400 degrees. Line a baking sheet with parchment paper. Using a 6-inch round cookie cutter, cut 6 disks of pastry dough. Prick the disks all over with a fork. Spread 2 tablespoons of applesauce on each disk, leaving a ¼-inch border along the outside edge. Lay the apple slices down like a fan, making sure that they overlap. Sprinkle apples with sugar and drizzle with butter. Bake for 10 minutes, rotate baking sheet 180 degrees and continue to bake for another 10 minutes. Serve warm, with a scoop of vanilla ice cream. **Makes 6 tarts.**

For apple-shaped tarts, use an apple-shaped cookie cutter approximately 4 inches in diameter to cut dough. Follow instructions above, but reduce the amount of applesauce to 1 tablespoon per tart and sprinkle each with a scant teaspoon of sugar and ½ teaspoon of melted butter. **Makes 8 tarts.**

More is More Chocolate Soufflé Tart

FOR CRUST:

¼ cup finely ground almond meal flour

¼ cup granulated sugar

2 tbsp dark brown sugar, firmly packed

3 tbsp Dutch cocoa powder

1 cup all-purpose flour

Pinch salt

8 tbsp unsalted butter

2 tbsp heavy cream

1 large egg yolk

FOR FILLING:

7 oz bittersweet chocolate, chopped

12 tbsp unsalted butter

⅛ cup white rum

4 large eggs, separated

½ cup granulated sugar, divided

¼ cup dark brown sugar, firmly packed

FOR CHOCOLATE SAUCE:

1 whole soft vanilla bean

¼ cup whole milk

1 cup heavy cream

8 oz bittersweet chocolate

2 tbsp unsalted butter

1 tbsp Dutch cocoa powder

Preheat oven to 350 degrees. Grease a 10-inch springform pan.

FOR THE CRUST: In food processor, mix almond meal, granulated sugar, brown sugar, cocoa powder, flour and salt. Chop in butter until it forms a coarse crumb. Add egg yolk and cream and mix. Scrape sides and gather dough together—it will be very sticky. Press dough into bottom and partially up the sides of prepared pan. Bake approximately 10 minutes, until barely baked. Let cool.

FOR THE FILLING: In the top of a double broiler, melt chocolate, butter and rum together. Use an electric mixer to beat egg whites with ¼ cup of granulated sugar until soft peaks form. In a separate bowl, whisk egg yolks with remaining ¼ cup granulated sugar and the brown sugar until lemon colored. Fold chocolate mixture into egg yolk mixture, then gently fold into beaten egg whites, being careful not to overmix. Pour into prepared crust. Bake for 10 minutes, turn 180 degrees and bake for another 10 minutes—the center should still jiggle a bit. Remove from oven and cool in pan on wire rack before removing rim. Serve with chocolate sauce (recipe follows).

NOTE: Tart can be made 1 day ahead and kept covered in the pan at room temperature until ready to serve.

FOR THE SAUCE: Split vanilla bean and scrape seeds into medium saucepan. Add milk and cream and bring to a boil, then remove from heat. Whisk in chocolate and butter and stir until melted. Strain chocolate mixture through a fine mesh sieve. Cool, cover and chill until ready to use. Reheat before serving. **Serves 14–16.**

Index